Waiting on Washington

Waiting on Washington

Central American Workers in the Nation's Capital

Terry A. Repak

Temple University Press
Philadelphia

Temple University Press, Philadelphia 19122
Copyright © 1995 by Temple University. All rights reserved
Published 1995
Printed in the United States of America

Design by Erin Kirk New

Library of Congress Cataloging-in-Publication Data
Repak, Terry A., 1953–
    Waiting on Washington : Central American workers in the
nation's capital / Terry A. Repak.
        p.   cm.
    Includes bibliographical references and index.
    ISBN 1-56639-301-9 (alk. paper). — ISBN 1-56639-302-7
(pbk. alk. paper)
    1. Alien labor, Latin American—Washington (D.C.)
2. Central Americans—Washington (D.C.)   3. Washington
(D.C.)—Emigration and immigration.   4. Central America—
Emigration and immigration.   I. Title.
HD8085.W183R46   1995
331.6'27280753—dc20   94-38120

For Stefan

Contents

List of Tables, Maps, and Photographs

Tables

Maps

Photographs follow page 134

Acknowledgments

Without the help and support of many people, this project would never have come to fruition. In particular, Maria Patricia Fernandez-Kelly provided inspiration, encouragement throughout, and practical advice for securing research grants. Peggy Barlett and Walter Adamson gave timely comments and keen insights as the project progressed. Thanks are also due to Robert Bach for his incisive critique of questionnaires and of sampling methods. Anne Statham generously gave her time and expertise to various versions of papers that have spun off from the analysis chapters. Demetrios Papademetriou, the former head of the Division of Immigration Policy and Research, U.S. Department of Labor, provided encouragement within a forum for discussion of the latest research on immigration at annual conferences. A research grant from this division, as well as a grant from the State University of New York's Institute for Research on Multiculturalism and International Labor (headed by Robert Bach), assisted in funding the research.

Numerous friends contributed their support and energy for various aspects of this project. Vilma Iraheta, herself a Salvadoran immigrant to the United States, accompanied me on many field-research expeditions and was an invaluable mediator during the interviews. She enriched the project immensely with her knowledge of the Central American community, her network of contacts, and her friendship with me. Rhina Martinez, Lyn Penniman, Steve Specter, Carol Squire-Diomandé, and Andrew Passen offered words of wisdom, information, and occasionally hands-on help. Anabela Garcia's photographs added an invaluable dimension, as did Doris Braendel's and Jenny French's editorial suggestions. Stefan Wiktor aided me in ways too numerous to recount, including the design of the research, the airing of ideas and plans, analysis of data, and editorial comments on all drafts of the chapters. Peter and Beverly Repak and Anna Wiktor entertained our children Adam and Halina for many hours when work demanded, and I am wholly indebted to my family.

Portions of the text of this book originally appeared in two articles by the author: "Labor Market Incorporation of Central American Immigrants in Washington, D.C.," *Social Problems* 41, no. 1 (1994): 114–28 (© 1994 by the Society for the Study of Social Problems—reprinted by permission); and "Labor Recruitment and the Lure of the Capital: Central American Women in Washington, D.C.," *Gender and Society* 8, no. 4 (1994): 507–24 (copyright © 1994 by Sociologists for Women in Society. Reprinted by permission of Sage Publications, Inc.).

Waiting on Washington

One

Introduction

Washington, D.C., is the seat of government, where laws are crafted to define which citizens of foreign countries are allowed to live and work in the United States. The city is also headquarters for the Immigration and Naturalization Service (INS) and other enforcement agencies that were established to keep all other people out of the country. Nevertheless, by 1990 Washington had become a safe haven and home to tens of thousands of undocumented immigrants. The city's largest and most visible immigrant community, numbering over 200,000 men, women, and children, originated in El Salvador and several other Central American countries. Within a single generation, Washington could claim the second largest settlement (after Los Angeles) of citizens from El Salvador in the United States and the third largest community of Central Americans overall.[1]

The peculiarities of the Central American migration to Washington are numerous. Before the 1960s, the nation's capital had never attracted international migrants in great numbers, and no particular national-origin group had ever predominated in the city. Indeed, only 7 percent of Washington's population was foreign-born in 1900, when as many as 37 percent of New York City's residents originated overseas. Washington's proportion of foreign-born residents dropped to a low of 4.2 percent at the time of the 1960 census but began to climb dramatically in ensuing decades. By 1988, at least 12 percent of Washington's population was foreign-born.

Foremost among the idiosyncracies of the Central American migration to Washington is the fact that women pioneered the migration in the 1960s and 1970s, when the city still lacked a substantial Latin American community and an international labor force. By comparison, cities in Texas and California drew a predominance of men among immigrants from Mexico, source of the largest number of legal as well as undocumented immigrants to the United States. Women constituted a slim majority among early Central and South American immigrants to Los Angeles and other cities in the United States; but among the initiators of the movement to Washington in the 1960s and 1970s, 70 percent of Central and South American immigrants were women.[2]

Ironically, it was employees of the U.S. government and of international agencies such as the World Bank and the International Monetary Fund who helped to instigate the migration stream that eventually brought tens of thousands of undocumented immigrants into the capital city. The life histories related in this book confirm that Washington's diplomatic, international, and professional workforce deliberately recruited many of the original Central American immigrants when they invited Central American women to work for them as housekeepers and child-care providers. These life histories issue from a study of Central American immigrants that included in-depth interviews with fifty Central American women and men (contacted primarily through social service agencies), a larger randomized survey of one hundred Central American households, and interviews with thirty representatives of social service agencies as well as with seventy-five major employers of foreign-born workers in the Washington area.[3]

The story of Rosa Lopez's family illustrates the diverse forces that lured many Central Americans to the Washington area in recent decades.[4] Rosa Lopez initiated a family migration that would eventually draw thirty-five other family members to settle in the Washington area. Rosa was a Salvadoran woman who worked as a housekeeper for a family from the U.S. Agency for International Development (USAID) when they were stationed in San Salvador in the 1960s. When the family's tour of duty was finished, they invited Rosa to return with them to Washington and continue working as their housekeeper. Once there, the family sponsored Rosa so that she could become a permanent resident of the United States, and soon she was able to send money to bring her husband, Javier, to Washington as well. Javier arrived in 1968 and found a job as a tailor in one of Washington's exclusive men's stores. In 1971 Javier and Rosa invited his niece Teresa (who was working as a domestic servant in San Salvador) to join them. Another American family that was seeking household help asked Rosa if she knew of any candidates for the position, and in this way Rosa arranged a job for Teresa. After eight years working as a live-in housekeeper for various families in the Washington suburbs, Teresa moved into her own apartment with a companion and had a son.

In 1980 Javier and Rosa learned that two other nieces were unable to find work in San Salvador. Eva was forced to abandon her studies because the university was shut down by the government when the civil war escalated. An attractive and articulate young woman, Eva was frustrated because in her attempts to locate a job in El Salvador she had been repulsed by the blatant sexual advances of prospective employers. She felt that her opportunities to secure employment without sexual harassment would be better in the United States even if she had to work as a maid. Similarly, her cousin Carmen lost her job in 1980 when the factory where she worked as a dressmaker closed because of the increased fighting in San Salvador. Like their cousin Teresa, both Eva and Carmen were single women with few prospects for gainful employment in El Salvador, and all three made the decision to migrate without the permission or aid of fathers or spouses. After securing their passage to the United States, Rosa arranged a job for Eva as a live-in housekeeper with an American family (who agreed to sponsor her as a permanent resident), and she allowed Carmen to live with her for a year while Carmen cleaned houses. Carmen found most of her daily housecleaning jobs through Rosa's network of friends. Eva invited her fiancé from San Salvador to join her once she became a permanent resident, and Carmen in turn brought her sister (with her three children) and two brothers to Washington.

Rosa's career trajectory is similar to that of other Central American women who gravitated to Washington at the invitation of employers who needed the services of domestic workers. Many of these women initially worked for diplomatic families that resided in San Salvador, Guatemala City, or one of the other Central American capitals. Among those who left their homelands to fashion new lives for themselves, a majority were single women like Teresa, Carmen, and Eva in the Lopez family or single mothers in Isabel Martinez's situation.

Isabel was proud of her English and animated by the opportunity to use her newly acquired tongue when she answered telephones at the downtown Washington social service agency where she worked. She also preferred to speak in English about her journey to the United States in 1975 and about the relocations that altered the course of her life. She left her small town in rural El Salvador to escape a partner who physically abused her and openly spent his money on other women. She resolved to rebuild her life elsewhere and to rescue her daughters from suffering the same fate as she. Without informing anyone but her mother, she spirited her two daughters out of town one day and hired a "coyote" (a person who helps smuggle undocumented aliens over the border) to drive them to Tijuana in Mexico. She paid $300 apiece for herself and the children to cross the border, but they were apprehended in Tijuana by immigration officials and sent all the way back to El Salvador. The next time she attempted to make the crossing she first flew with her daughters to the U.S.-Mexican border and then, with the help of a coyote, slipped across through tunnels at night.

Isabel lived in Los Angeles with only her daughters until her brother joined her six months later. She worked for a while as a live-in housekeeper and then for one year in a dry cleaner's. She was content with her new life in Los Angeles because she enjoyed the temperate climate and was able to establish friendships quickly within the large Latin American community there. But when she and her brother learned from friends that there were more jobs, with better wages, in Washington, D.C., they decided to relocate to the East Coast. After settling in Washington with her daughters, Isabel contacted a woman originally from her home town who knew her mother, and with the woman's help she secured a job as a dishwasher in an Italian restaurant. But Isabel earned only $75 for a grueling fifty-hour work week and soon left that job to work in a Latin American grocery. Six months later she took a job as a housekeeper in a hotel, where she remained for several years until she met and married a Guatemalan man named Luis.

Like Isabel, Luis also had a high school degree when in 1968 he journeyed to Washington at the invitation of his sister. At the time, his sister was a housekeeper for a diplomatic couple from Guatemala stationed in Washington, and she helped him secure a position as a cook in a Latin American restaurant. He worked there for a number of years and then shifted over to a Chinese restaurant, still employed as a cook. After five years wrapping egg rolls and concocting stir-fry dishes night after night in the same restaurant, he still earned only $5 an hour. Even though he was a permanent resident and could command higher wages elsewhere, Luis's shy and genteel nature kept him from pressuring his employers for raises. Isabel, the more ambitious partner, worked at the same restaurant as her husband until she received her green card. Then she quit her job, enrolled in an English-language instruction class at a community center, and later landed a position as a receptionist at a social service agency. She is very proud of the fact that she no longer has to clean other people's houses or tend their children and that she can work in her profession as a secretary, speaking English much of the day.

Isabel's narrative is remarkable in a number of senses. First, she was a single mother who made the decision to uproot her family and journey to the United States without the permission or assistance of a father or husband. Second, both she and her husband had been raised in the urban middle classes of their countries of origin and there had finished high school. Third, she found all her jobs through other women and their gender-based social networks. While Isabel and her brother were living in Los Angeles, they learned through social networks that a smaller city three thousand miles away on the East Coast could offer them better jobs with higher salaries. Labor recruitment had prompted Luis's sister to move to Washington to work as a housekeeper for a diplomatic family.

As seen in these family histories, women were favored in the recruitment efforts by Washington's diplomatic and professional families in need of housekeepers and child-care providers. The initial immigrants in two of the three families described above were women who were "recruited" to work by employers in the Washington area. To a large extent the movement of Central American immigrants to the Washington area unfolded in two stages. Women such as Rosa, Isabel, and Luis's sister predominated in the early migration stream in the 1960s and 1970s, when over two-thirds of Central and South American immigrants to Washington were women. The migration pattern shifted in the 1980s, when wars in El Salvador, Guatemala, and Nicaragua sped the departure of more men from those countries than previously.

One of the major implications of these findings is that Latin American migrations should hardly be viewed as a homogeneous phenomenon. Gender-based migrations evolve with specific socioeconomic circumstances in both sending and receiving countries, and they in turn beget unique sets of consequences and ripple effects. This examination of the Central American migration to Washington incorporates gender as an essential element in the migration process and creates opportunities for new perspectives on old themes in the migration literature. A focus on gender helps to elucidate the motivations behind the large-scale emigration of Salvadorans, Guatemalans, and Nicaraguans from their countries during the latter decades of the twentieth century. Gender issues also explain why many Central Americans chose to move to a city like Washington, D.C., even though it lacked a large Latin American population and well-established community services to accommodate new immigrants. The life histories recounted in this book illustrate the extent to which informal or "gendered" labor recruitment and the establishment of gender-based social networks operated as determining factors in the decision to migrate and the eventual choice of destination. They also reveal the unusual degree of autonomy demonstrated by Central American women in all facets of the migration process. These themes evolve in the subsequent chapters as gender differences for Central American immigrants are scrutinized in four critical areas of the migration process: in the formulation of migration strategies; in labor force participation patterns and experiences in the workplace; in measuring the impact of new immigration laws on recent immigrants (specifically the Immigration Reform and Control Act of 1986, or IRCA); and in gauging changes in relationships and gender roles that accompany migration and settlement in the United States.

For years the migration literature ignored women because of the assumption that men predominate in movements of people across borders. Many early studies of immigration even used the word "migrant" to refer exclusively to men, and "their families" was shorthand for dependents (i.e., wives and children). Stereotypes derived from the study of immigrant men were meant to suffice as a basis for descriptions of immigrant women's experiences. Women were somewhat simplistically depicted as dependents who waited in their countries of origin before passively following their husbands to other countries, even though women have outnumbered men among legal immigrants to the United States for the last half century. From 1930 to 1979, women accounted for 55 percent of legal immigration and outnumbered male immigrants by over a million. Similarly, for decades women have outnumbered men in rural-to-urban migrations within most of the Latin American countries.[5] These trends demonstrate that women's roles in labor migrations are fundamental and vital and that accurate portrayals of their experiences can hardly be derived from formulas based on conceptions of immigrants as men.

Forces That Propel International Labor Migrations

This treatment of the Central American migration to Washington, D.C., relies on the framework of historical-structural theory to explicate the myriad forces that propel and direct labor migrations. Historical-structural theory stresses the economic connections of an integrated world as well as an international division of labor. Highlighting the interrelationship between labor markets in the United States and in other countries, it abandons the simplistic "push-pull" model and that model's narrow focus on individual motivations for migration. Instead, historical-structural theory describes how the gradual development of an international economic system resulted in a growing interdependence among nations and regions. Using this model, earlier studies have demonstrated how the advance of capitalism in less developed societies produces or accentuates social and economic imbalances that result in outward migration, generally to areas from which the original investments of capital emanated.[6]

One fundamental premise of the historical-structural perspective is that employers who must search for new sources of low-cost labor have the option of either exporting the production process to countries where such labor sources are located (as many U.S. firms have) or importing low-cost labor to replace the domestic workforce. Businesses such as agricultural or service-oriented enterprises, which are unable to export themselves abroad, become prime employers of immigrant labor in the United States. This is particularly valid in cities where jobs in services predominate, such as in Washington, D.C., a city that never spawned production-and-assembly jobs that could later be exported to other countries. Since the 1960s the overall shift in the U.S. economy from a manufacturing base to a service-oriented economy has accelerated the demand for low-wage labor. The emergence of "world cities," or centers that coordinate global economic activities, has further accentuated the need for new low-wage labor sources. With the spread of residential and commercial gentrification as well, immigrant communities have sprung up to fill the ever-expanding pool of service jobs available. As Saskia Sassen-Koob explains, "There is, then, a correspondence between the kinds of jobs that are growing in the economy generally and in major cities particularly, and the composition of immigration—largely from low-wage countries and with a majority of women."[7] Other studies have underlined the gender-specific nature of many labor migrations by demonstrating that women constitute an increasing proportion of recent immigrants to the United States due to the structural transformations in the global economy. For example, women have become the preferred labor force in the export manufacturing plants along the Mexican border as well as in California's garment and electronics firms, just as they have been for years in domestic service.[8]

Social and economic conditions in immigrant-sending countries influence the gender-specific nature of different labor migrations and determine whether more women or more men are available or impelled to migrate longer distances for work. Structural conditions in Ireland in the latter part of the nineteenth century, for example, dictated that women had few opportunities for employment or for marriage in that country. The availability of domestic-service jobs in the United States and the channeling of young women through kin-mediated chain migration brought more Irish women than men to the United States for decades. Cultural norms in immigrant-sending countries—especially those related to marriage—also facilitate the predominance of women in certain migrations. As Katharine Donato noted, "Women who live in nations that espouse nonlegal unions may not face the legal responsibilities incurred by marriage and may be freer than women from other countries to cross international borders."[9] The following chapter delineates how structural conditions such as low marriage rates and the gender composition of households in countries like El Salvador and Guatemala allowed women the flexibility to accept jobs as domestic workers and child-care providers in countries like the United States.

In a similar vein, particular structural conditions in receiving countries, such as the availability of domestic-service and child-care positions, may be more conducive to women's migration than to men's. Many women are attracted by such labor opportunities, and knowledge of their availability provides an important stimulus for migration. Demand in the United States for domestic servants and changes in U.S. immigration laws after 1965 made it easier for women than for men to obtain labor certification (i.e., work authorization) in certain job categories. Jamaican women, for example, predominated over men in the early migration stream to New York for these reasons.[10] Whereas Chapter Two portrays a major immigrant-sending country (El Salvador), Chapter Three describes the circumstances and structural conditions that transformed Washington, D.C., into one of the newest and largest immigrant-receiving cities in the United States.

Historical-structural theory may account for the overall social and economic circumstances in immigrant-sending and -receiving countries that delimit the flow of migrants, but the model is inadequate without the necessary linkage to microlevel explanations. Chapter Four introduces a concept termed *gendered labor recruitment,* which provides the link between macro- and microlevels of analysis to explain the peculiar direction of certain migrations such as the movement of Central Americans to Washington, D.C. Structural factors set the stage for a surge in Central American migration but gendered labor recruitment affected the timing and direction of the movement to the nation's capital.

Labor recruitment theory explains how certain migrations result from the deliberate recruitment of particular groups of workers. According to this perspective, employers actively seek out workers with specific characteristics who are willing to relocate, and thus stimulate migrations to certain areas. The original immigrants then form the basis for social networks, which influence the decision about destinations for new migrants and reinforce migration flows to particular points.[11] Labor recruitment theory implies a major organized effort on the part of employers to advertise for and recruit large groups of workers. In the twentieth century, active labor recruitment to the United States is best exemplified by the *bracero* program, which brought Mexican workers to farms and fields in the Southwest. Government-paid agents scoured Mexico during and after the Second World War in order to recruit workers, and at its conclusion in 1964 the *bracero* program was responsible for bringing approximately five million workers into the country.

A more informal type of labor recruitment explains why many of the initial Central American immigrants to the Washington area chose that city as a destination even though it lacked a well-established Latin American community. As many of the life histories related in subsequent chapters demonstrate, Washington's government, diplomatic, and professional workforce actually recruited or invited many foreign workers to accompany them to the nation's capital. A vanguard of Central American immigrants—predominantly women in the 1960s and 1970s—laid the basis for the social networks that eventually expedited the migration and settlement of a second wave of Central Americans into the Washington area in the 1980s. While Central American women composed the most desirable labor pool to employers seeking housekeepers, child-care providers, and cleaning staff,

Central American men eventually learned about the surfeit of jobs in construction, landscaping, and janitorial services through these networks.

The role of social networks in the regulation of migrant flows and in the early survival of new arrivals has already received a great deal of attention.[12] Most of the literature, however, has ignored the gender-based character of these networks because of the presumption that men predominated in international labor migrations. Since the theoretical models described above focus primarily on the institutional features of labor migrations, they fail to account for the gender-specific circumstances and choices that women and men face. Immigrants are too often portrayed as compliant nonentities in their responses to structural forces, just as they once were said to be "pushed" or "pulled" into immigrant "streams." Any analysis of migration as a social process must take into account the ways in which gender shapes and constrains migration decisions. "It is the immediate context of family and community relations which determine how people will respond to pressures exerted by structural transformations," as Pierrette Hondagneu-Sotelo observed.[13]

Labor Market Experiences upon Migration

While the aforementioned theories also inform the debate over the labor market experiences of immigrants once they settle in the United States, they again fail to identify and explain critical gender differences in this area. The following personal histories provide a glimpse at how gender dovetails with structural factors to determine the occupational "success" and employment mobility of Central American immigrants in Washington, D.C. Structural factors may account for men's advantageous wage levels and employment mobility, but gender constraints are preeminent in the basic divisions of the U.S. labor market and in wage scales in general.

A recent migrant from El Salvador, Marina Suarez enjoyed her work as a counselor at a social service agency in downtown Washington. She easily established rapport with her clients—most of whom were from El Salvador and Guatemala—as she counseled them and reassured them that there were many channels for locating jobs in Washington. With a university degree in education, Marina had been a high school teacher in San Salvador before she left the country for an "extended vacation." Several years before her migration, her brother Bernave and mother had moved to Washington when Bernave learned about the plethora of construction jobs in that city. Marina decided to join her family in Washington for a year or two in order to care for her ailing mother and to leave behind her the daily trauma of working in war-torn El Salvador. Upon arrival in Washington, she initially found daytime housecleaning jobs through her mother's and brother's networks of friends. One of her clients was a lawyer at a legal assistance firm for Latin American immigrants, and this lawyer told Marina about a counseling position at a social service agency when there was an opening available. Marina applied, and was overjoyed when she was selected for the position. Although she labored with an overload of clients at the social service agency for three years, she still earned only $350 per week (or $8.75 per hour). In fact, her salary was the same as one of the housekeepers she helped place in a downtown Washington hotel—a woman who had completed only three years of school before leaving El Salvador. In contrast, Marina's brother Bernave, who has a ninth-grade education, has been able to move up the ranks in his construction company from a starting position as a laborer to that of a skilled carpenter. He earns $650 a week, almost twice what Marina makes.

In general, immigrant men in Washington are able to ascend a more tangible career ladder and achieve economic "success" more quickly than immigrant women from Central American countries. Monico Hernandez, for example, came to the United States in 1981 when the fighting in El Salvador escalated, because he did not want to be drafted into the army. He was seventeen years old and had completed eleven years in school. At first Monico lived with his sister in Los Angeles and worked there for several years at landscaping and painting jobs. But when he heard that there were more jobs and higher wages in Washington, D.C., he moved east on his own. He lived with a cousin and for three years worked as a painter with his cousin's group of friends, earning $8 per hour (or $320 weekly)—almost twice what he had been earning in Los Angeles. After applying for permanent residency under the amnesty program, he enrolled in English-language classes and began to look for more stable employment. In 1989 he received his green card, and by then he spoke English well enough to secure a position as an engineer with a U.S. government agency at a starting salary of $18 per hour (or $720 weekly). Monico had five fewer years of education than Marina Suarez, and yet he earned more than twice what she did.

The debate over immigrant economic incorporation in U.S. labor markets also pits historical-structural theorists against proponents of assimilation theory (with its "human capital" model). The human capital model posits that personal characteristics of immigrants—such as their level of education, English-language ability, length of time in the United States, and legal status—are the most important factors determining occupational "success" and employment mobility in the United States. For example, in comparing the earnings of foreign and native-born adult white *men*, Barry Chiswick showed that although immigrants initially earn less than the native-born, their earnings rise more rapidly with U.S. labor market experience. After ten to fifteen years their earnings equal and then exceed those of the native-born. George Borjas's work confirmed that, on the whole, the earnings of Hispanic immigrant *men* increase with time since migration. Cordelia Reimers attributed a Cuban-Anglo wage differential also to personal characteristics, that is, to length of time in the United States and knowledge of English.[14]

More recent studies question the assimilationist theory that with sufficient time in the United States immigrants will eventually fare as well as native-born groups.[15] Historical-structuralists challenge the concept that individual characteristics of immigrants are the main determinants of earnings, because the notion ignores the importance of structural arrangements in the work place. Instead, they predict that workers in the primary labor market (generally those employed in large or multinational companies) will receive higher wages than employees in the secondary market (associated with smaller, more competitive firms), and that income differences will persist regardless of individual skills and traits. Two characteristics of the secondary labor market that affect wage levels are that jobs are unstable and that they are predominantly held by minorities.[16]

Historical-structural theory proposes that structural factors in the economy—particularly the sector of employment (e.g., construction, restaurant, or service industries)—are more critical determinants of wage levels and employment mobility than are any personal characteristics of workers. However, because relatively few studies have explored the ways in which women's labor market experiences vary according to the above-mentioned variables described for men, these models ignore gender-based differences in factors that determine wage levels and economic "success." In one study that analyzed data from the 1976 Survey of Income and Education and made general comparisons between all Anglo and all Hispanic-origin employed women, education level emerged as the greatest influence on occupational status for Hispanic women. After this human capital trait, structural characteristics (i.e., sector of employment and ethnic composition of the labor market) constituted the second determinant of socioeconomic status for Hispanic-origin and Anglo women. Language proficiency emerged as a strong influence on occupational allocation for Central and South American women, the group that had the lowest levels of English fluency. More recently a case study of the Chinese enclave in New York City stressed the structure of the labor market—that is, hours worked and sector of employment—as having the most consistent effect on women's earnings. The study noted that women who work in enclave economies in particular are highly exploited and that none of the human capital variables (education, English-language proficiency, or citizenship) affect earnings.[17]

The findings presented here broaden the debate about immigrant economic incorporation by assessing the factors that account for differences in Central American men's and women's wage levels and employment mobility. This analysis carefully considers the problem of gendered patterns in labor market incorporation and proposes that gender issues, in conjunction with the structural context in which international migrants labor, are the paramount influence on wage levels and employment mobility. Because the migration experiences of men and women differ dramatically, gender plays a forceful role in determining how rapidly immigrants are incorporated into area labor markets, how well they perform financially, and whether they experience any mobility into higher-status jobs with better wages. For immigrant women, the labor market in the Washington area tends to be polarized between low-skilled poorly-paid jobs (e.g., in domestic service) and high-skilled white-collar jobs—which are often poorly remunerated as well. Immigrant men, on the other hand, generally encounter employment opportunities and wage levels that range across a broader spectrum. The career trajectories of individuals like Marina Suarez, her brother Bernave, and Monico Hernandez illustrate these trends. Chapter Five describes the structural peculiarities of service-oriented economies such as Washington's and sheds more light on the distinctions between women's and men's experiences in these labor markets.

The Variegated Impact of New Immigration Laws

The state, as "gatekeeper," regulates migration flows by formulating and then attempting to enforce immigration laws, usually in conjunction with domestic and foreign policy concerns and ostensibly without intending to discriminate. Changes in U.S. immigration law since 1965 aimed to redress earlier laws that discriminated heavily against certain national-origin groups, although realistically the laws still reflect conflicts between groups in the United States that benefit from immigration (such as agricultural employers) and groups that do not. Policies concerning refugees also tend to reflect biases in U.S. foreign policy interests. Throughout the 1980s (during the Reagan-Bush administrations), the government granted asylum to a majority of applicants who were fleeing from Communist countries (such as Cuba), while denying refugee status to those fleeing from countries that were nominally sympathetic to the United States.[18] For example, the percentages of people granted political asylum from countries with governments hostile to the United States were quite high—such as those from Iran (60 percent) and Poland (35 percent)—whereas fewer than 3 percent of those who fled from El Salvador at the height of the civil war in the 1980s were granted political asylum.[19]

When certain groups are designated political refugees (as Cubans and Vietnamese were in the 1980s), the government provides an array of resources—such as housing subsidies, job training, English-language instruction, and medical care—that are not available to other immigrants. On the other hand, a hostile reception by the U.S. government forces immigrants into an underground existence and makes incorporation into the receiving society more laborious and tentative.[20] The vast majority of Central Americans who made their way to cities in the United States in recent decades were unauthorized immigrants who had to search for work and otherwise fend for themselves while hiding their identities from the authorities.

Congress passed the Immigration Reform and Control Act of 1986 specifically to stanch the flow of undocumented immigrants over U.S. borders by imposing fines on employers who knowingly hired unauthorized workers. Although lawmakers may not have intended for IRCA to discriminate against any groups on the basis of sex or national origin, the research indicates that this may indeed have been one of the outcomes. By setting the cut-off date for the general amnesty program at January 1, 1982, for example, the government rendered ineligible for permanent residency under the program a majority of those who came to the United States fleeing civil wars in El Salvador, Nicaragua, and Guatemala in the 1980s. In effect, Central American immigrants were welcome to enter the United States by invitation only, when their labor was needed to tend the houses and children of the elite in Washington and in other cities, but not when their lives were threatened by civil wars.

IRCA succeeded in making the settlement process more tedious for unauthorized immigrants because job seekers first had to secure documentation (fraudulent or otherwise) before locating employment in the United States. But the evidence presented in Chapter Six suggests that IRCA has done little to deter immigrants from entering the United States or from returning once they are deported. Generally, within the six months to a year after IRCA became law, most undocumented immigrants as well as their employers were able to devise ways to circumvent or to ignore the law, whereas others merely tolerated and complied with its dictates. IRCA clearly did not pose an impossible barrier to employment for undocumented immigrants in the Washington area, as the 3 percent unemployment rate among Central Americans in 1988 and 1989 indicated. But it may have had a subtle effect on the gender balance of migration flows. Responses from the Central Americans surveyed in Washington as well as from employer interviews indicate that immigrant women are able to secure employment more easily than immigrant men since the passage of IRCA.[21]

IRCA had less short-term impact on employment patterns for Central American women than on those for men in the Washington area. More women testified that they took only glancing notice of the law when it went into effect, while more men complained about the negative reverberations throughout their work and family lives. A majority of the surveyed Central Americans who claimed that employers never asked them to produce work permits or other legal documents were women. Few private individuals who employed domestic workers (predominantly women) felt compelled to fire them after the passage of IRCA, whereas work conditions were less stable for immigrant men. The recession that gripped even the thriving Washington area after 1989 further exacerbated problems with employment, housing, and economic survival that the undocumented (who have no access to public funds when the job market shrinks) must negotiate. The repercussions felt by families and households from recent changes in U.S. immigration laws are sharply differentiated on the basis of gender, as Chapter Six documents.

Shifting Roles for Men and Women

In Washington, unequal wage scales distinguishing Central American women from men reflect gender-based segregation in U.S. labor markets in general and a bias that places lower value on women's labor than on men's. The diversity in migration and work experiences for women and men incites profound alterations in gender roles and identities, and Chapter Seven tracks the ways in which these diverse migration experiences reverberate in the work/family nexus. One of the most striking features to emerge from lengthy interviews with Central American women and men was the unusual degree of autonomy demonstrated by Central American women in the decision-making stages of the migration process. Over two-thirds of the women interviewed claimed to have made the decision to emigrate on their own, without the collaboration or assistance of male partners or fathers. This is a marked contrast with earlier Mexican and Dominican migration patterns, in which women tended to migrate after men in order to reunite the family.[22]

Other studies have described how the balance of power between men and women in households shifts upon migration as women gain greater personal autonomy, independence, and decision-making leverage from their participation in the labor market and in community life. Men, on the other hand, are forced after migration to share authority, decision-making, and sometimes even household responsibilities (albeit unevenly) with women, particularly if women are employed full-time outside the home.[23] Central American women in Washington display an array of responses to their altered circumstances upon migration. These immigrant women view themselves as primary actors and independent decision makers in the timing of their migration and the choice of their destination; a majority were already active participants in the wage-labor force in their countries of origin. The women I interviewed spoke openly about their perceptions of changes in women's and men's roles upon migration to and settlement in the United States. The consensus among them was that women attain far more independence and freedom in the United States than they could realize in their countries of origin, but that they pay dearly for these rights by having to work harder than they did at home and often at jobs below their skill levels, juggling full-time work with family responsibilities. Because many of the women were single at the time of their migration or had been abandoned by partners and were left with children to support, few of them became dependent on partners to the extent that they needed men to mediate the host society for them.

The interviews also reveal how conflicts that women experienced in their relationships with men intensified as many of the values the women were raised with, such as connection and cooperation in the family and community, were superseded by "first-world" values like freedom, growth, and individual achievement. Both women and men agreed that relationships became more complicated and contentious as they attempted to relate to each other under altered conditions. A woman's sense of autonomy and changes in the allocation of household responsibilities were in many cases difficult for men to accept. Women's wage-labor participation clearly remains an essential element in strategies for survival because most families in the Washington area are unable to survive on one provider's salary. Chapter Seven describes the tensions that arise when transplanted couples and families attempt to regroup, reform and formalize relationships in an alien culture. The divided emotions expressed by both men and women about their newly complicated relationships are hardly unique to Central American immigrants. In many senses these recent immigrants articulate the poignant mix of bittersweet blessings that all transplanted individuals experience upon migration to a new country.

Two

Portrait of a Central American Sending Country

Despite a long tradition of migration within and between the Central American countries, the recent pattern in which men *and* women migrate to more distant countries (such as the United States) is a relatively new phenomenon. The smallest and most densely populated country in the western hemisphere, El Salvador was not a major exporter of emigrants to the United States in earlier decades. In actual numbers it ranked behind Costa Rica, Guatemala, and Honduras in the 1960s, when just 15,000 Salvadorans legally entered the United States. That figure leaped tenfold within a generation as 134,400 Salvadorans officially entered the United States in the 1980s (see Table 1). The numbers of undocumented Salvadorans who crossed the border into the United States may be almost ten times the number of legal entrants. Although unauthorized immigration is impossible to measure, recent studies estimate that as many as one million Salvadorans and half as many Guatemalans were living in the United States in the latter part of the 1980s.[1]

What accounts for this massive displacement and movement of people from North America's nearest neighbors within a single generation? While political turmoil and civil war shattered El

Table 1   Country of Birth of Legal Immigrants to the United States,
1961 to 1989 (in thousands)

Country of Birth	1961–70	1971–80	1981–89
Costa Rica	17.4	12.1	12.7
El Salvador	15.0	34.4	134.4
Guatemala	15.4	25.6	55.6
Honduras	15.5	17.2	37.5
Nicaragua	10.1	13.0	32.5

Source: U.S. Department of Commerce, Bureau of the Census, *Statistical Abstract of the United States* (1991).

Salvador's economy in the 1980s, the same confluence of forces to varying degrees resounded throughout other Central American countries. Combinations of violent civil strife, political repression, high population-growth rates, a concentration of land in the hands of wealthy families, and sharp declines in commodity prices (and internal production) devastated the economies of El Salvador, Nicaragua, and Guatemala. Recent Central American migration patterns, which issue from a complex melange of causes, attest to the futility of insisting upon a precise demarcation between "economic" and "political" motivations for migration.

The historical-structural framework explains migration as a major consequence of capitalist development; when countries at a lower level of development are incorporated into the world economy, penetration by foreign or domestic capital causes disruptions in traditional modes of production and exchange. Dramatic economic changes and dislocations sometimes even lead to political conflict or revolution. Migration is one response to these economic dislocations and to changes in the world economy as people are forced to find new ways to earn a livelihood and to provide for their families. Cultural penetration, particularly through the media and the dissemination of commercial products, also enhances the incentive to migrate to more developed countries, where standards of living are perceived to be higher and more attractive.[2] People move in search of work, in response to direct labor recruitment, or with more subtle incentives provided by indirect labor recruitment and family networks.

Gender adds another critical (although often overlooked) element to understanding the ebb and flow of entire communities, households, and individuals across national borders. Structural characteristics of the Central American sending countries compel certain members of households to migrate in search of work or of domiciles where they might live in peace. Similarly, structural ties to and characteristics of labor markets in particular receiving cities may hold more allure for women than for men among those who wish to emigrate. Cultural norms also foster a gender bias in many migrations from major sending countries. Donato (1992:170), for example, noted that "countries reporting consensual marriages [i.e., not legally sanctioned] offer women greater opportunities than other nations to leave and migrate to the United States." In the same vein, cultural norms in receiving societies determine whether women or men are preferred as candidates for certain jobs—such as housekeeping or child-care positions.

This chapter delineates the historical-structural features of a major Central American sending country and links them with the sociocultural conditions that facilitate or preclude gendered migrations. It examines the factors that set the stage for the recent displacements and migrations within the Central American countries, focusing on El Salvador in particular. El Salvador is the source of the largest immigrant population in the Washington, D.C., area, of the largest Central American immigrant population in the United States, and of the second-highest number of unauthorized immigrants (after Mexicans) apprehended nationwide by the Immigration and Naturalization Service.[3]

Land Concentration and Emigration

El Salvador first became a republic in 1821 after it (along with the other Central American territories) declared its independence from Spain. But El Salvador emerged as a modern nation-state and entered the world economy in the late nineteenth century only when its inhabitants first began to cultivate the coffee crop. Before ambitious farmers seized upon this cash crop, a relatively harmonious division of the land existed between cattle-raising hacienda owners and crop-growing villagers who cultivated primarily maize. Between 1880 and 1912, middle- and upper-class families bought up the common lands of the villages in the fertile volcanic hills in order to cultivate coffee trees on a more lucrative scale. Land concentration transferred more and more land to fewer and fewer hands, to the point that fourteen families, having consolidated their hold on the best lands in the country, emerged to form a ruling oligarchy. The government conspired in this endeavor by passing laws that eliminated or reduced communal lands and expropriated church properties.

Migration rates accelerated as land concentration intensified. Peasants who lost their lands were able to continue farming only by squatting on unused land on coffee estates or by migrating to other (generally marginal) regions of the country.[4] Coffee cultivators employed large numbers of workers primarily at harvest time, a practice that had a momentous impact on migration patterns, since it encouraged the growth of a mobile rural sector of seasonal workers. The cyclical patterns whereby peasants mi-

grate in search of employment on the coffee estates between November and March continue to this day. The same patterns also
evolved in the banana-growing countries Guatemala, Nicaragua,
and Honduras. The introduction of cotton as a major cash crop
in the 1950s forced even more permanent employees and small
cultivators to rely on seasonal work, often through migration.

The number of jobs in the agricultural sector plunged when
farmers began to adopt modern mechanization techniques in the
1950s, and by the end of that decade landless peasants and seasonal workers constituted a majority of the rural population (64
percent). In El Salvador, ten hectares was said to be the minimum
amount of land required to support an average family.[5] Yet by
1971 land concentration was so severe that only 5 percent of
agricultural families held ten hectares or more and 16 percent
held between two and ten hectares. While a majority of rural
families had become migrant workers with less than one hectare
of land or none at all, six families possessed as much land as 80
percent of the rural population together. This pattern of land
concentration had a more profound impact on the agricultural
population of El Salvador than did rapid population growth;
William Durham's 1979 study showed that over three-fourths of
all migrants originated from the excluded population of landless
and land-poor peasants. A smaller middle strata of peasants who
turned their plows to the cultivation of sugarcane coalesced by
the late 1960s, but by 1966 coffee monopolized nearly half of
the arable land dedicated to El Salvador's principal crops. Coffee, cotton, and sugarcane displaced important food crops like
corn, rice and beans, and few Salvadorans derived any notable
benefits from the export crops.

The changing configurations of land ownership and seasonal
employment also had a profound effect on family structures and
on the gender division of labor in these societies.[6] As more and
more peasants abandoned subsistence farming for paid agricultural labor (e.g., for seasonal work on coffee plantations), men
were preferred as wage workers, while women were relegated to

informal-sector activities. Women's farm labor and other under-takings (such as the production of handicrafts) remained unpaid or poorly remunerated. As in most Latin American countries to-day, agricultural labor no longer offered a viable market for women's labor in El Salvador. When the introduction of tech-nological innovations further displaced labor, more women be-gan to migrate to urban areas in search of work to supplement the seasonal agricultural work of men. In some Central Ameri-can countries cultural norms also compelled daughters to leave the family home at a certain age, since generally women were ex-cluded from inheritance rights. If they did not marry, then daughters were forced to enter the labor market, and this transi-tion was easiest to effect in an urban setting. Dora Orlansky and Silvia Dubrovsky (1978:9) noted that "migration at a younger age is one of the few channels for upward social mobility avail-able to single rural women in the lower socioeconomic levels." Sons, on the other hand, found greater employment opportuni-ties in rural areas than daughters, since they might work in per-manent or in seasonal jobs.

Cities offered more opportunities for wage work to women largely because of the availability of domestic-service jobs. Do-mestic service was a "typical labor market" for migrant women be-cause few men in Latin America competed for jobs in this sector. It was also a labor market generated by the supply of labor, since "the abundant flow of women in the younger age groups who are driven out of rural areas makes actual a potential demand."[7] Is-abel Nieves's 1979 study noted that 34 percent of urban women and only 10.5 percent of rural women in El Salvador actually worked for a salary. (The first figure was probably an underesti-mate because of the difficulty in counting women who work in the informal sector.) While urban women were paid less, they found work more easily than did men and tended to have more economic security. Nieves noted that in El Salvador "women's diminished economic dependence on their spouses under these circumstances helps explain the proliferation of household groups formed by women with children to support but no stable partner."[8] Several studies highlighted the fact that large numbers of households in El Salvador formed "free unions" instead of legal marriages (about 50 percent), and that nearly 40 percent of households among the urban poor were headed by women.[9] El Salvador has had one of the lowest marriage rates in the hemisphere partly because both men and women were forced to migrate for work and because there was little purpose among the lower classes to secure inheritance through marriage. For these reasons it has been acceptable (and financially essential) for women to migrate greater distances for work—particularly if they were abandoned by partners and were left with children to support.

Women were definitively excluded from paid agricultural work after 1965, when the government instituted a minimum-wage policy, which led many estate owners to stop hiring women or to classify them as minors and pay them 20 percent less than men. Many poor farmers who had lost their land, as well as women who were unable to find paid employment in the agricultural sector, had no recourse but to search for work in the cities of El Salvador or to migrate across state borders.[10] While women tended to migrate to urban areas (to San Salvador in particular), many men had traversed the border into neighboring Honduras when that country experienced a boom in commercial agriculture in the 1950s, as well as into Guatemala and Nicaragua for work on cotton plantations. The Salvadorans who had migrated illegally to Honduras in the 1950s were later expelled during the so-called Soccer War between Honduras and El Salvador in 1968.[11] Legal immigrants to the United States had numbered less than 50,000 from all of the Central American countries in the decade 1951–60. But in subsequent decades, when political discord and state repression escalated in the region, qualitative changes in migration patterns occurred as the numbers of people moving across borders expanded exponentially.

Broadening structural and economic ties between the United States and its Central American neighbors created new forces that would generate migrations in a different direction. In the aftermath of the Cuban Revolution in 1959, U.S. foreign policy was focused on reinforcing the nascent Christian Democratic party in El Salvador as a means of countering the influence of the Left on political developments in the hemisphere. Throughout the 1960s, the United States sought to strengthen economic ties with El Salvador by supporting the economic integration of the Central American countries under the rubric of a Central American Common Market (CACM). The U.S. Alliance for Progress boosted development by funding construction of schools, homes, health facilities, and water projects. Numerous companies based in the United States also established "offshore production plants" for assembling and packaging imported components in El Salvador and in neighboring countries, which enabled them to pay extremely low wages and to avoid the encumbrances of labor unions. Women were sometimes the preferred labor force in these factories, particularly in the clothing and textile industries, where they eventually composed 70 percent and 37 percent of the workforces respectively.[12] These broadening structural ties further contributed to the out-migration of people from both cities and countryside as they became familiar with North American commodities, work routines, and wages. Several Central American women interviewed in Washington, for example, claimed that they had worked for U.S.-owned factories in their countries of origin before they migrated to the United States for work. While these various forces helped to encourage out-migration from Central American countries, simultaneous transitions in the U.S. economy proved increasingly attractive to a low-wage immigrant labor force and to women in particular, as the following chapter details.

Political Polarization and Emigration

A number of Latin American countries have sustained long personal dictatorships where one man ruled for years through the military (such as Somoza in Nicaragua or Stroessner in Paraguay). But El Salvador boasts the longest-running and most in-stitutionalized military rule in Latin America because the military has been the focal point of political power throughout most of the twentieth century.[13] A peasant uprising earlier in this century helped to cement a profitable partnership between the oligarchy and the army. Led by Farabundo Marti, the son of a mestizo landholder, the unorganized and poorly coordinated uprising was brutally suppressed by the army, and in 1931, 30,000 peasants were massacred.[14] *La matanza* (or "the massacre") forced many peasants and Indians to flee their homes and generated a great wave of migration to Honduras and to other parts of the country. After the uprising the army and the oligarchy coalesced into an invincible ruling force in El Salvador. To ensure that its interests would be protected by the state, the oligarchy fashioned a spoils system in which it rewarded key army officers with money, land, and business investments.[15]

From 1932 to 1979, six different coups traumatized the country, although power merely shifted among conservative factions in the military because the Communist party and all peasant organizations were banned and trade union activity was discouraged. Since formal power centered in the military for many decades, joining the army became one of the few career paths to upward mobility for young men. As Marvin Gettleman and his colleagues (1986) explain, peasant conscripts and draftees from the urban underclasses filled the lower ranks of the army in exchange for regular pay and freedom from agricultural toil, for relief from destitution and direct exploitation. "Thus the army served to keep a lid on popular discontent inherent in a system that functioned to enrich the dominant oligarchies and their allies, but by the 1960s social forces that were impossible to contain became manifest."[16]

The succession of anti-Communist colonels and generals who governed El Salvador throughout the 1960s and 1970s contributed to the polarization of Salvadoran society and precipitated new waves of migration. Particularly in the countryside, conflict between leftist factions and rightist supporters of the status quo grew intractable in the course of the latter decade. The military attempted to win over major segments of the agricultural population by encouraging people to join a large paramilitary and antirevolutionary organization in the countryside called the Organización Democratica Nacionalista (ORDEN). The organization offered peasants such "benefits" as favorable credit terms and full-time employment and arranged hospital beds and schools for family members. In turn ORDEN members supervised their villages and reported any inclinations toward leftist support or subversion among their neighbors. In 1970 ORDEN's network of informers and collaborators numbered between 60,000 and 100,000—almost two-tenths of the entire rural population.[17]

Events came to a head in 1979, when a group of reformist army officers who blamed the unrest in the countryside on the government's intransigence over agrarian and social reforms staged a coup. They formed a junta with the declared intention of promoting basic reform in the agrarian and financial systems and of guaranteeing freedom of speech, press, assembly, and trade union organization. Although military leaders agreed to make modest agrarian reforms, the oligarchy protested and put a halt to the junta's proposals. The junta was forced to proclaim a state of emergency and to ban all meetings of more than three people. Faced with internal divisions and with pressure from more left-wing organizations to adopt reform policies opposed by the right wing, the junta fell apart. At the end of 1979 the armed forces launched a terror campaign that claimed the lives of hundreds of people. Leaders of various popular organizations in El Salvador responded by calling a joint press conference and announcing the creation of the Revolutionary Coordination of the Masses. The organizations then staged the largest demonstration in El Salvador's history as over 200,000 people marched in the streets of the capital. After soldiers, police, and paramilitary units fired on the demonstrators and killed forty-nine civilians, the popular organizations turned to preparations for civil war. They won wide-ranging support from many sectors—including officials and professors of the Jesuit-run University of Central America and members of the clergy, led by Archbishop Oscar Arnulfo Romero.

When Defense Minister Jose Garcia assumed command of the government in 1980, terror campaigns against all opposition groups spilled over to envelop apolitical citizens in the cities and countryside and generated the largest displacement and outmigration of men and women in the country's history. Members of the security and military forces (as well as the landowning oligarchy) formed death squads that targeted peasant leaders, union members, teachers, and clergy who agitated for reform. Young people were coerced into joining either the army or insurgent forces, and farmers and villagers were forced at gunpoint to choose sides as well, as some of these Salvadoran men and women interviewed in Washington later testified.

> I was afraid for my children. One day the army came to my house and a soldier put his gun against the head of my oldest son to force him to go along with them.

> Every time I had to go by bus to San Salvador to sell my machetes, the police would inspect the buses. They were suspicious of me and threw me in jail. Then when I was at home, the guerrillas would come to the house and steal my machetes.

> Men were being drafted by the army or the guerrillas, and there were often people dead on the streets. The army killed twenty-five people in my neighborhood.

> I was the commandant in my town, and many people from the town who were my friends were among the guerrillas. Two of my cousins who were in the army were killed by the guerrillas, and I was in a difficult situation. I decided to desert from the army and go to the United States to live in peace.

In the 1980s political polarization prompted the exodus of many young men who hoped to avoid being drafted by either side in the struggle or who were sent abroad by mothers seeking to protect their sons. But women also became targets of political repression and death threats because they were joining the insurgents in increasing numbers and augmenting their social activities by organizing in villages and in the cities (as students, teachers, or trade union members). Especially in the towns and cities, the middle and working classes tended to follow Christian Democratic or Social Democratic parties at the "liberal" end of the political spectrum, and labor unions became quite vocal in agitating for economic reform.

In the countryside, death squads terrorized members of the newly established farm cooperatives and shot leaders who participated in land reform programs. (Years later a United Nations investigation accused the Salvadoran armed forces of committing or condoning flagrant abuses of authority to a degree that distinguished the Salvadoran struggle from other wars of this era.)[18] Even the Catholic Church became a highly visible target of human rights violations. Seventeen priests, nuns, and religious workers were killed between 1981 and 1984 alone because church members helped thousands of individuals and families who were persecuted, subjected to death threats, or suspected of leftist political activity to leave the country (partly through the Sanctuary Movement).[19]

Throughout the 1980s the terror campaign mounted as the army began making sweeps of guerrilla-controlled areas, particularly in El Salvador's northern provinces of Chalatenango and Morazan. Human rights organizations accused the Salvadoran armed forces of perpetrating massacres of entire villages during these campaigns so that the FMLN would be left without rural support.[20] The "year of terror" (1980) culminated with Archbishop Romero's assassination by right-wing agents as he was celebrating mass in San Salvador, followed by the brutal rapes and murders of four North American churchwomen by a right-wing death squad.[21] Testimony from those who made their way to the United States corroborated accounts of the pernicious terror campaign against unarmed citizens from 1980 onward. A number of individuals interviewed for this book related such experiences after they were conducted to safety by the Sanctuary Movement.

Patricia Valle, for example, a mother of five, endured several years of death threats before she fled from Morazan Province in 1983. When a local death squad accused her partner of being a guerrilla sympathizer, he slipped across the border into Mexico knowing that assassins were searching for him. The night two men came to the house asking for him, Patricia was alone with her children. The men sent the children out of the house, then raped and beat her and seared her lips and hands with burning cigarettes, repeatedly demanding that she divulge the whereabouts of her partner. As the men prepared to leave the house, they warned Patricia that she had ten days to flee the area before she would be killed.

The next morning several neighbors visited her to offer sympathy and presents for the journey while she packed her bags and prepared to take the children to Mexico. Patricia had no trouble locating someone who was familiar with the border area and who would agree to drive her and her children into Guatemala. But the men who had come to her house the previous night were waiting for her as she left town with her escort. They flagged the car down, bound the eyes of Patricia and her children, and forced the driver to take them to a deserted farm nearby. Six men from the death squad were waiting in the house, and they forced Patricia to undress and then raped her in front of the children. When they finished, they asked her what her final wish was, and she begged them to kill the children immediately rather than subject them to torture. As one of her daughters tried to approach her, several men yanked the girl out of the room. Patricia became so frightened for her daughter that she lost consciousness. When she awoke, she presumed that her children were dead, until she felt her daughter touch her and heard her say, "I'm alive, I'm alive!" Then she learned that a local woman had informed the authorities of their whereabouts and that policemen from the town had frightened the death squad agents away. The authorities instructed Patricia's driver to take her to the capital (San Salvador), but instead he acquiesced to her pleas and drove her to the border with Guatemala. For eight days she and her children made their way across that country by hitchhiking, and then they crossed the border into Mexico.

After five more days of travel, she arrived in Mexico City and found her partner, who failed to recognize her because of the burns and bruises on her face. The children in turn refused to acknowledge their father, and Patricia realized how much damage the assaults had caused them. She took the children to psychologists at the University of Mexico, where for two years they were treated at a psychiatric institute. At the time the devastating earthquake struck Mexico City in 1985, Patricia and her husband were living in a refugee community aided by the Sanctuary Movement. They lost all of their belongings and their jobs because of the earthquake, but Sanctuary slipped Patricia's family to safety into the United States via the new underground railroad. The movement financed their passage to Washington, where Patricia's brothers and sister were already living. Once settled in that city she sought and found a job with a refugee assistance organization in order to help others like herself.

Another Salvadoran woman in Washington related how her husband, a political leader in San Salvador, was forcibly abducted from their home late one night, never to be seen alive again. Several other women were teachers who had fled from El Salvador after close colleagues were murdered or "disappeared" (shorthand for those who were kidnapped and never seen again). The teachers claimed that they were easy targets for political persecution because even glib or innocent statements uttered in their classrooms could be interpreted as criticism of the status quo (ergo they would be accused of disseminating leftist propaganda). As the war intensified and spread to all of El Salvador's provinces in the 1980s, military offensives included massive bombing and strafing in certain areas where crops and homes were targeted for destruction. Waves of peasants from the rural areas were displaced and hounded into exile, along with union leaders, teachers, students, and activists from urban areas.

In this way the pace and composition of earlier migration patterns changed considerably by the late 1970s, when growing numbers of educated and professional women and men were forced to leave their homes for personal safety as well as for economic survival (see Table 2). For example, Central Americans formed a more recent and faster growing immigrant stream— with an older age structure, a sex ratio favoring women at all ages, and higher education levels, occupational status, and English-language proficiency—than that of Mexican immigrants to the United States. Steven Wallace's 1986 study found that almost half the adult Central Americans living in California in 1980 had completed high school (versus less than a quarter of Mexican immigrants) and that 25 percent had attended college. Close to one-third of Central Americans (and only 9 percent of Mexicans) had worked in white-collar occupations in their countries of origin.[22]

"Economic" Versus "Political" Motivations for Emigration

When full-scale civil war erupted in 1980, President Ronald Reagan was determined to stave off a revolution in El Salvador that would compound his humiliation over the Sandinista victory in Nicaragua. Under U.S. pressure, Christian Democrat Jose Napoleon Duarte was allowed to remain in the government in 1982 even though ARENA and other right-wing parties formed a majority coalition in the Assembly. In return, the United States agreed to increase economic and military aid. At least 75 percent of the $1.7 billion sent to El Salvador between 1981 and 1985

Table 2   Migration Data for Washington Area Respondents

	Survey Sample* (N=100)	Interview Sample (N=50)
Sex of respondents:	(Number)	
Men	57	17
Women	43	33
Country of origin:	(Percent)	
El Salvador	60	86
Guatemala	18	6
Nicaragua	11	8
Honduras	9	
Panama	2	
	(Years)	
Average age	33.5	32
Average education	7.7	9.5
English-speaking ability:	(Percent)	
Good	14	52
Fair	18	10
None or poor	68	38

*"Survey Sample" refers to the larger sample of 100 Central American households.

involved war-related money or materials. By the early 1980s El Salvador had become the third largest recipient of U.S. aid worldwide, after Israel and Egypt. The Reagan administration subsequently asked Congress to approve $8 billion in economic aid alone over the five-year period from 1984 to 1989. The funds were contingent upon the administration's guarantee that the government in El Salvador made progress in controlling human rights abuses, in improving economic performance, and in winning the war against the guerrillas.[23]

The billions of dollars in U.S. economic and military aid sent to El Salvador did little to improve the quality of life for the

(continued)

	Survey Sample (N=100)	Interview Sample (N=50)
Year departed origin country:	(Percent)	
1960–69	3	2
1970–79	11	24
1980–81	19	32
1982–85	41	22
1986–89	26	20
Total after amnesty cutoff	67	42
Year arrived in United States:		
1960–79	8	26
1980–81	10	26
1982–85	40	22
1986–89	42	26
Total after amnesty cutoff	82	48
Legal Status:		
Undocumented	50	34
Permanent residents	19	24
Amnesty applicants	20	42
Political asylum applicants	11	

lower classes; more Salvadorans were living in abject poverty than at any time in the twentieth century. By 1983, with unemployment hovering around 40 percent in the city (60 percent when combined with underemployment, and 90 percent in certain rural areas), a majority of Salvadorans were barely able to provide the minimum daily food requirements for their families. A USAID study conducted in 1988 found that only one in ten Salvadoran peasants had access to safe drinking water, whereas in 1984 that ratio had been three in ten. As a result, infant mortality rates soared, while American aid (which provided close to

55 percent of the national budget) continued to cushion the effects of the war for the upper and middle classes and to sustain economic growth. Per capita income was among the lowest in Latin America ($470 in 1983), and the literacy rate in 1978 stood at only 50 percent in urban areas and 30 percent in rural areas.[24]

The Salvadoran economy eventually collapsed under the pressure of increased violence in the cities and in the countryside, leaving more and more people destitute. Employment in the industrial sector dropped as all of the industries in the tax-free zone in eastern San Salvador halted operations because of the fighting. Between 1979 and 1981 an estimated 330 industries closed down, greatly augmenting the numbers of unemployed workers who sought to leave the country. Women, who constituted over 40 percent of the industrial workforce, were generally the first to lose their jobs and were forced to invent work for themselves in the informal sector—in street vending or in domestic service. Women and men together faced massive unemployment without any government subsidies, since the country had never designed a social security system for the unemployed. Coffee production also declined during the early years of the war and the gross national product (GNP) fell 25 percent from 1979 to 1983—clearly indicating the extent to which war was ravaging the economy.[25]

Close to half of the Central American immigrants interviewed in the Washington area claimed that they fled their countries because of oppressive political conditions and civil strife. Even those who attributed their departures to unemployment and poverty blamed the civil war for exacerbating already difficult economic circumstances as factories and businesses were forced to close (see Table 3).[26] They claimed that due to the turmoil caused by the war, they were no longer able to support their families. As one man explained, "Because of the situation I felt very desperate living there, because there was no future." Another man insisted, "The civil war does not give me a chance to work,

Table 3   Reasons Respondents Gave for Leaving Their Countries of Origin (in percent)

			Both Samples	
	Survey Sample* (N=100)	Interview Sample (N=50)	Pre-1980 (N=27)	1980–84 (N=123)
Civil strife (total):	39	48	26	48
War, fighting in area	25	26	19	28
Personal injury, torture, death threats, persecution	14	22	7	20
Economic reasons (total):	38	16	37	31
Poor economic conditions or unable to find work	26	8	22	22
To improve opportunities or get better job and wages	12	8	15	9
Other (total):	23	36	37	21
To join relatives in U.S.	12	6	4	11
Miscellaneous reasons	11	30	33	10

* "Survey Sample" refers to the larger sample of 100 Central American households.

and I don't support either side." A third man testified, "Where I was farming, the guerrillas would come and ask for food. It was dangerous, and I could not cultivate any longer. There were always threats against me and my family."

Such responses demonstrate the futility of semantic debates over the demarcation between "economic" and "political" refugees from countries such as El Salvador, Guatemala, and Nicaragua. Throughout the 1980s, the Reagan and Bush administrations denied asylum to hundreds of thousands of Salvadorans and Guatemalans who were fleeing their countries, and justified the exclusion with the argument that they were "economic refugees," lumping them together with immigrants from Mexico and other Latin American countries. The facile classification of Central Americans as immigrants solely seeking better employment opportunities led to the denial of political asylum to more than 90 percent of those who applied for protection in the United States.[27] Yet in actuality "economic refugees" from Central American countries were rarely the victims of shifting or troubled economies alone.

While their motives for departure differed from those who could find no means to support themselves, members of the upper classes also chose to leave El Salvador during this period. The U.S. government's reception of wealthy Salvadorans was hardly as hostile as that accorded to the average "economic" immigrant from El Salvador. Between 150 and 300 families from the oligarchy took up residence in Miami by mid-1980 and established lobby groups to pressure the U.S. Congress for even more military and economic aid. Years later, the United Nations Truth Commission on El Salvador issued a report that chastised the United States government for allowing wealthy Salvadoran exiles a base in Miami for subversive operations. These exiles "helped administer death squad activities between 1980 and 1983 with apparently little attention from the U.S. government." Other news reports revealed that the Reagan administration knew more than it publicly disclosed about the exiles' connections with the military and right-wing death squads, and that the Reagan administration routinely withheld such information from the U.S. Congress.[28]

With growing resistance among the American public to U.S. support for the war in El Salvador, the U.S. Congress finally voted in 1991 to cut military aid to El Salvador. It authorized only half the requested amount of $95 million to be sent to the Salvadoran government, since no progress had been made in the investigation into the murders of six Jesuit priests in San Salvador the previous year. Eventually Alfredo Cristiani's conservative government was forced to negotiate an end to the war with the FMLN, and both parties signed a formal peace treaty in early 1992.[29] More than 75,000 people had died in the twelve-year-long civil war. Based on its investigation into the brutalities of the war, the United Nations Truth Commission on El Salvador charged that state security forces and allied death squads, which were linked to high-ranking army officers (including members of Cristiani's cabinet), had committed the bulk of the human rights abuses and violence. For example, the commission accused the late Roberto D'Aubuisson, the former army major who founded the ruling ARENA party, of ordering the assassination of Archbishop Romero. It also found that the five national guardsmen convicted of killing four American churchwomen in 1980 were obeying superior orders, and that a former defense minister knew the truth but covered it up during investigations. The report accused another former defense minister of ordering the murder of six Jesuit priests at the Central American University in 1989. It charged the FMLN with the execution of mayors in war zones, with planting land mines that claimed innocent victims, and with killing wounded prisoners. The Truth Commission called for the dismissal of all military officers (numbering over forty) and government officials cited for human rights abuses and recommended that they (along with several leaders of the insurgents) be banned from taking part in public and political life for ten years. With the demise of the Cold War, the defeat of the Sandinistas in Nicaragua, and a peace treaty in El Salvador, Central America has once again faded into the background of overall U.S. foreign policy concerns.

Migration Patterns Since the 1980s

In total, close to one-third of the entire population of El Salvador was displaced by war and related political-economic factors between 1978 and 1988, according to Segundo Montes Mozo and

Juan Jose Garcia Vasquez (1988). The same forces that inspired massive emigration from El Salvador also impelled increasing numbers of Guatemalans and Nicaraguans to migrate northward to the United States in the latter decades of the twentieth century. Guatemala, for example, has experienced the longest-running civil war of any country in Latin America, dating from 1954, when a military conspiracy (in collusion with the U.S. Central Intelligence Agency) ousted the popularly elected government of Jacobo Arbenz Guzman. As in El Salvador, army generals (along with the conservative elite) have been the de facto rulers in Guatemala, instituting a policy of strong political repression that has caused an exodus of Guatemalans in recent decades. Between 1978 and 1985, the military battled insurgents for control of the countryside and devastated the western highlands in the process. As Nora Hamilton and Norma Chinchilla (1991:95) noted, "government-instigated terrorism against opposition leaders in urban areas combined with a brutal counterinsurgency campaign against the Indian population that killed thousands and displaced hundreds of thousands." In total, approximately 38,000 people "disappeared" in Guatemala, and 100,000 people died during the decades of fighting. Over 40,000 officially recognized Guatemalan refugees fled into Mexico (with an unofficial total of 150,000) and many more émigrés moved farther north to Los Angeles, Houston, and other U.S. cities. In the early 1980s the fighting and an economic recession in Guatemala caused more than 400 industrial establishments to shut down operation and at least 10,000 industrial workers lost their jobs.[30]

Also during the 1980s, structural factors and natural forces colluded in generating the largest movement of people ever recorded out of Nicaragua, when an estimated 500,000 people (out of a population of 3.5 million) emigrated to neighboring countries. Initially, the ideological content and "authoritarian cast" of the Sandinista revolution inspired a politically motivated exodus of those associated with Somoza or members of the

upper class. Later, the young Sandinista government implemented a universal conscription law, which led to an exodus of
young men seeking to avoid the draft. The contra war and the
U.S. trade embargo imposed in 1985 further exacerbated the
general decline of the Nicaraguan economy, a decline manifest
in a rapid increase in the rate of inflation from 32 percent per
year (between 1980 and 1984) to 20,000 percent in 1988. The
war and related military actions to depopulate certain areas of
the country uprooted an estimated 200,000 families. Making
matters worse, Hurricane Joan displaced a further 300,000 people in 1988.[31] The Contadora Peace Accords, crafted by all five
Central American countries in 1987, brought peace two years
later, after the U.S. Congress cut military aid to the contras at the
end of 1988. With Violetta Chamorro's assumption of power in
1989, attention of U.S. foreign policy makers waned and subsequently shifted away from the area.

Apart from civil wars, the three major Central American sending countries shared a number of other structural characteristics
that promoted migration since the 1960s. First and foremost was
the shortage of land for poor farmers. The concentration of land
in the hands of wealthy families was an intractable problem in
Guatemala (e.g., 90 percent of the country's farms measured less
than seven hectares), and income distribution was almost as
skewed as in El Salvador. Land concentration had been a serious
problem in Nicaragua as well, but rural inequality was less pro-
nounced there than in El Salvador.[32] For a majority of people in
all three countries, the quality of life has been low compared
with neighboring Costa Rica. Infant mortality rates hovered
around 65 per 1,000 live births in El Salvador, Nicaragua, and
Guatemala, while Costa Rica's was 13.9 (see Table 4). In 1984,
76 percent of the population of Guatemala (approximately 6
million out of 8 million) was classified as poor, and life ex-
pectancy was only 56 years for urban Guatemalans and 41 for
those who lived in rural areas.[33]

In sum, the combined forces of political repression and civil

Table 4 Comparison of Demographic Data and Population Characteristics of Central American Countries

Country	1990 Population (in Millions)	% of Population in Each Age Category		Density (per km²)	Fertility Rate	Infant Mortality (per 1,000)	GDP*
		(0–14 yrs)	(15–64 yrs)				
Costa Rica	3	36.1	59.7	59	3.1	13.9	$4,870
El Salvador	5.2	43.7	52.7	250	4.2	64.0	1,890
Guatemala	9.2	45.2	51.8	84	5.4	46.6	2,920
Honduras	5.1	44.8	52.1	46	5.2	69.0	1,610
Nicaragua	3.9	45.9	51.5	30	5.3	62.0	n/a

* Per capita gross domestic product is reported in 1990 current international dollars.
Sources: United Nations Demographic Yearbook (New York: United Nations, 1990); World Bank, *World Development Report* (New York: Oxford University Press, 1992).

war, deteriorating economic conditions, natural causes (e.g., earthquakes and hurricanes), and burgeoning bonds with countries such as the United States (via social networks, media, and indirect labor recruitment) colluded in engendering the dramatic increase in emigration from these three Central American sending countries over the latter decades of the twentieth century. The landless and land-poor peasants who left El Salvador, Guatemala, and Nicaragua and migrated north in the 1960s and 1970s were joined by students, teachers, unemployed factory workers, activists, and victims of persecution or death threats in the late 1970s and 1980s. Multitudes of apolitical men and women who were caught between warring factions and ruined economies fled their countries to ensure the safety and survival of their families. As Hamilton and Chinchilla noted, "U.S. foreign policy appears to have been more effective in generating refugees than U.S. immigration and refugee policies have been in preventing their entry."[34]

Although these structural and political forces set migration processes in motion, gender played a preeminent role in the decision-making stages, in the composition of the migrations, and in the choice of destination points. The structural forces that propel migrations influence men and women differently, and numerous studies emphasize that women have predominated in rural-to-urban migrations throughout the countries of Latin American.[35] The situation in El Salvador succinctly demonstrates how women in rural areas are doubly disadvantaged by a lack of inheritance rights and a dearth of paid employment opportunities for them—compared with those for men—in the agricultural sector. Cyclical migration for work contributed to the disintegration of the family in El Salvador, as evidenced by the low percentages of marriages and legitimate births among households in that country. The migration of relatively young people during the war years further aggravated the problem of family disintegration because the general trend is for migrants to form new relationships wherever they establish residence. Since a large proportion of migrants leave children and spouses behind, the result is (at least temporarily) a rupture in families.[36]

When war and economic crisis forced factories and other businesses to close, women were often the first to lose their jobs. Many of the women who chose to leave El Salvador and neighboring Central American countries altogether and to seek employment abroad were abandoned by partners and left with small children to support. The gender composition of many households in El Salvador and cultural acceptance of the notion that women could migrate for work meant that women were available to take jobs as domestic workers and child-care providers in the United States in the 1960s and in subsequent decades. When news about favorable living conditions and an abundance of jobs in U.S. cities such as Washington, D.C., reached large and small Central American towns, many candidates for these jobs risked the journey and the possibility of detention in order to grasp an opportunity to live and work in peace.

Three

Portrait of a U.S. Receiving City

      Only in recent decades, as increasing numbers of Central Americans were leaving their countries because of internal wars, human rights abuses, and economic hardship, has Washington, D.C., become a magnet for international migrants. The nation's capital held few attractions for immigrants in the nineteenth and early twentieth centuries—especially in comparison with other large American cities—because it was not a major port for oceangoing ships and because passengers could not debark there easily. Washington was considered a backward country town lacking the size and dynamism of New York, Boston, Philadelphia, and Baltimore. Little heavy industry existed in the capital area, and most available jobs were government related and inaccessible to foreigners. In 1900, a year in which 37 percent of the population of New York (and 35 percent of Boston's population) was foreign-born, the District of Columbia counted only 7 percent of its residents as foreign-born.[1]

But the character of the city changed dramatically in the second half of the twentieth century just as the composition of its population did. Once a very segregated Southern city renowned for its intolerable sweltering summers, Washington has evolved into an international metropolis with most major businesses and international organizations maintaining at least representational offices there. Since 1960, the influx of immigrants has coincided with a stunning cultural and economic transformation in the city. By 1990 it was home to over half a million immigrants, many of them undocumented, who found that the nation's capital provided a safe haven and a place to earn a lucrative livelihood. Figures on the numbers of Central Americans (and Salvadorans in particular) in the Washington area vary widely because so many of them are recent arrivals and because of the difficulty in counting a largely undocumented population. In 1987, the *Washington Post* estimated that 80,000 Salvadorans lived in the District and 100,000 more resided in the surrounding suburbs (see Map 1).[2] When combined with the figures for Guatemalans, Nicaraguans, and Hondurans, the numbers of Central American immigrants in the nation's capital may reach well over 200,000.

Just as gender plays a central role in the decision to migrate from one country to another (as well as in the composition of a migration), it is also a decisive factor when immigrants cast about for destination points in the United States. Characteristics of various labor markets in receiving cities hold different allures for women and men, particularly in a city replete with service-sector jobs, such as Washington, D.C. The rapid expansion of gender-specific jobs—such as child care and domestic service in the 1960s and 1970s—clearly held more attraction for immigrant women than for immigrant men. This chapter renders a portrait of the nation's capital in order to highlight the gender-based structural characteristics that lured particular groups of immigrants in large numbers. The trajectory of Central American immigrants in Washington is juxtaposed with that of African Americans in the region's labor markets, since the city's peculiar regional development pattern provided an abundance of different jobs for both groups.

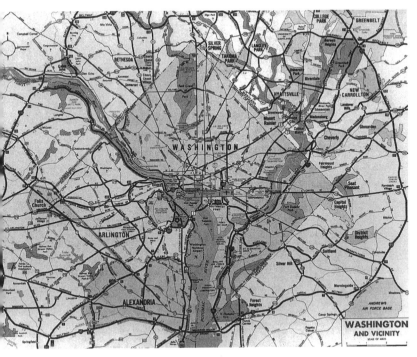

Map 1 The Washington, D.C., metropolitan area. From the *Delaware, Maryland, Virginia and West Virginia Road Map 1993*. Used by permission of the publisher, H. M. Gousha/a division of Simon & Schuster, New York.

Transformations in an Emerging World City

Washington's legacy as the nation's capital and a politically planned city has haunted its inhabitants since it was founded. Because it functioned originally as a government center, it earned the erroneous reputation early on of being an "unreal" city, without factories or immigrants or subways and with a population that largely changed with each new national government.

Another stereotype, that the city was an oasis for African Americans, evolved during the Civil War era, when the District of Columbia first emerged as a critical administrative and military center.[3] Former and runaway slaves fleeing the South migrated to the city as did throngs of soldiers who were billeted in Washington during the Civil War and remained there after its conclusion. In the twentieth century, further expansion of the federal government proceeded at an exponential rate on account of two world wars. Franklin Roosevelt's Washington was a thoroughly segregated Southern town in which most hotels, restaurants, movie theaters, libraries, and taxi cabs refused to serve African Americans. At the onset of the Second World War, African Americans composed about a third of the city's population, and more migrants from the tobacco lands of Virginia and North Carolina streamed into the area daily.[4] The newcomers had little contact with the already established black middle class residing in the better neighborhoods, since they were forced to wedge their families into alleyways and hastily erected shanties.

When in the early 1940s war brought boom times to Washington, the city's population increased at a rate of more than 50,000 a year. Most new arrivals to the city sought employment, and in the labor-starved capital jobs were easier to find than elsewhere in the country. The federal government, for example, employed some 200,000 whites at the onset of the Second World War, but by 1943 the Civil Service Commission petitioned Congress for an additional 500,000 employees.[5] The regional labor market also offered a profusion of jobs that were low-wage or gender-specific (e.g., secretarial and service-oriented positions), drawing African Americans and women in large numbers. The federal government actually engaged in a form of labor recruitment during this period, targeting women in particular by advertising in local newspapers around the country for patriotic workers—especially women who could type—to move to Washington for work. The ads drew tens of thousands of young women, who eventually became known as "government girls."

As David Brinkley (1989:107) wrote, "They came on every train and bus, nearly all of them women, wearing dyed-to-match sweaters and skirts and carrying suitcases tied shut with white cotton clothesline. . . . If you could type and had a high school diploma, you were hired. $1440 a year."

The Second World War transformed Washington in other ways as government spending burgeoned and business concerns from around the country dispatched representatives and lobbyists to the nation's capital. Washington began to bill itself as the capital of the free world, and the federal government's expansion attracted legions of lawyers, lobbyists, journalists, consultants, think tanks, and diplomats. The numbers of international immigrants to the Washington area also began to swell after World War II. Europeans initially predominated among legal immigrants because of the entrance of war brides, refugees, and persons displaced from Eastern European countries. A modest number of Cubans found their way to Washington in the 1950s and 1960s, most of them arriving after Castro's assumption of power, and they opened the first Cuban restaurant in the Adams Morgan section of the city (see Map 2). Asians who were admitted as refugees, particularly those from South Korea and Indochina, came in large numbers in subsequent decades. Most of these migrations ensued from internal wars around the world, such as the consolidation of North and South Vietnam, the Soviet presence in Afghanistan, and the overthrow of Haile Selassie in Ethiopia and of the shah in Iran. By the mid-1980s Washington was home to the third largest concentration of Central Americans in the United States, the fourth largest group of Koreans, and the largest group of Ethiopians outside of Africa. In 1990 the INS ranked Washington sixth among major metropolitan areas in the number of immigrants it attracted. Until recently no particular group of immigrants predominated in the city, but since 1980 the numbers of Central Americans have multiplied most rapidly.

Washington is now a superb example of an emergent "world

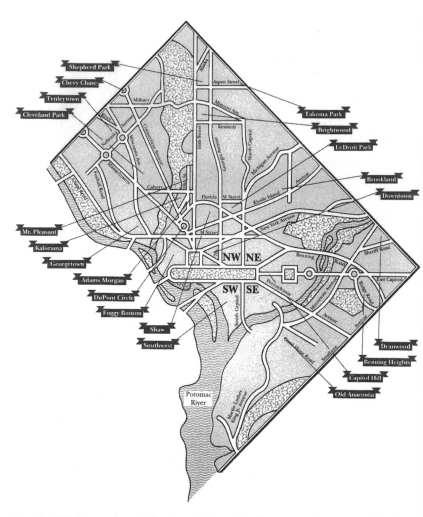

Map 2 Washington's neighborhoods. From *Washington at Home: Neighborhoods in the Nation's Capital,* p. 6. Used by permission of Windsor Publications, Inc.

city," or a central point from which global economic activities are coordinated.[6] But the city maintains its distinction from other major urban centers of the United States, where the shift in recent decades from an industrial base to service-oriented industries resulted in an increase in the number of high-skilled jobs overall as well as an expansion of low-skilled and semiskilled jobs. Washington was never a center of production or manufacturing and did not undergo the structural transformation from a goods-producing to a service economy typical of other large cities in the United States. Instead, its rapid emergence as a world city is due largely to population gains, the process of gentrification, and the growth of service industries, biotechnology firms, research-and-development concerns, and consulting companies. An explosion of small businesses in the capital area generated new jobs at a rate 50 percent higher than the national average in the 1980s, making Washington's one of the strongest economies in the country during that decade. The federal government has always contributed to the economic stability in the area because of the large number of jobs it generates (one in six area workers hold government jobs). At the end of 1988, Washington's economy was ranked the fourth healthiest in the country, as measured by the Grant Thornton Index. Because of employment gains in the service and construction sectors, the rate of expansion of the Washington economy trailed only that of San Diego, Minneapolis, and Atlanta in the three previous years.[7]

As a result, Washington has experienced chronic labor shortages since the 1970s, when the area's economic boom first began generating jobs faster than the population could fill them. From 1970 to 1980, for example, the region grew by 210,000 people at a time when over 490,000 jobs were added to the economy. From 1983 to 1988 the population increased by 12 percent and jobs by 27 percent.[8] Population growth rates shot up in the 1980s, and by 1988 the metropolitan area held over 3.7 million people. Conversely, unemployment rates declined to a low of 2.9

percent in the District of Columbia in 1988 and hovered around 1.9 percent in several of the surrounding suburbs. Area demographers noted in 1989 that the Washington area had the tightest labor supply of sixteen major metropolitan areas.

A number of features distinguished the Washington metropolitan area from other major urban centers in the United States. With its large professional population, Washington led the nation in income and education levels in the 1980s. In 1985 the Washington metropolitan area was home to the five richest counties in the United States, based on per capita income (excluding Loving, Texas, a county with large cattle ranches and only a hundred inhabitants).[9] Washington was also home to the most highly educated population in the nation: 80 percent of adults over 25 had completed 12 or more years in school and 51 percent had attended college. The city ranked first in the proportion of technical and professional employees in its labor force and had more scientists and engineers per capita than any other metropolitan area. This surfeit of professionals has earned Washington the reputation for being a "yuppie town," and gentrification in the region has required an army of low-wage workers to provide specialty services and child care for the many two-career families residing there.

The Gender-Segregated D.C. Labor Market

Foremost among Washington's distinguishing characteristics is the proportion of women who participate in the wage labor force. The ratio, which is 69 percent of women sixteen years of age and older, is the highest in the nation and 22 percent higher than the national average. Washington-area women entered the workforce in unprecedented numbers after 1970, a year in which only 45 percent of women aged sixteen and older worked outside the home. By 1986 the proportion of women in the workforce had jumped to 69 percent. The massive entry of women into the wage-labor force generated escalating demand for yet more women who could tend the children and households of Washington's wage-earning families.

When Washington-area women sought to enter or return to the wage-labor force in large numbers, they found few feasible solutions for their child-care dilemmas because of the dramatic shift out of the domestic-service and child-care industries by African American women after 1960 (when the U.S. Civil Rights Act opened up clerical jobs to African Americans). The high percentage of African American women who were private-household workers in 1960 (37.5 percent nationwide) plummeted by the end of the 1980s, when only 3.5 percent of employed African American women still worked in domestic service. The move out of service and into clerical occupations enabled African American women to improve their occupational distribution to such an extent that their median income increased from 51 percent of white women's income in 1955 to 98 percent in 1975.[10] Clearly, child- and elder-care industries and domestic service involved such long hours and poor pay (with few benefits and little opportunity for advancement) that these occupational sectors could no longer attract a stable domestic workforce. Indeed, the salaries of household child-care workers ranked lowest of all occupations tracked by the Bureau of Labor Statistics, at $8,008 in 1992.

With little government interest or community assistance in alleviating their child-care problems, many professional couples turned to immigrant labor to fill the vacuum for domestic workers and child-care providers. Washingtonians eventually recruited enough private-household workers that by 1992 at least 11 percent of children under the age of five received in-home child care, double the U.S. census figure of 5.3 nationwide. Because informal-sector jobs are generally underreported in census data, the actual proportion of children receiving in-home care may exceed 11 percent. According to immigration lawyer

Michael Maggio, "Washington, D.C. almost certainly has more undocumented nannies and household workers than anywhere else in the country."[11]

The dearth of child-care providers and domestic workers has forced many Washington women who wish to participate in the wage-labor force to remain at home. Professional Washington couples who can afford the fees often turn to nanny agencies to solve their child-care dilemmas. Among the estimated one thousand nanny agencies in operation throughout the country, the highest concentration is on the East Coast. Agencies in Washington that secure nannies and housekeepers maintain long lists of families waiting for child-care providers even though many of the families on the lists are willing to sponsor foreign-born workers for labor certification. One manager of a large nanny agency in Washington remarked in an interview that at any given time she had three hundred families on her waiting list for domestic help. She explained, "We used to have a lot of African American women who would call in the past, but they don't call anymore. Either they don't go through agencies, or they have other opportunities for work now." The employer estimated that live-in nannies with legal documents could earn $300 to $400 per week (in 1990), while undocumented immigrants earned around $200 weekly. Most child-care providers are paid in cash (off the record) and receive no medical, vacation, or sick-leave benefits.

Although nanny agencies do refer many foreign-born workers to families seeking housekeepers and child-care providers, a majority of Latin American women (particularly those who are undocumented) use their own private networks or the social service agencies in order to secure such positions. A registered nurse living in Washington who wished to return to work part-time claimed that she languished on the waiting list at a nanny agency for two years, hoping to find a child-care provider for her four children. The nanny agency sent six candidates to her over the course of many months, but most of them were uninterested in making the long commute to the suburb where the family resided. One candidate spoke little English and another insisted she would have to return to her country for an extended visit later that year, so that eventually the potential employer decided to abandon her search and stay out of the job market indefinitely. On the other hand, another Washington employer (a lawyer) interviewed in Washington claimed that she was able to return to work soon after the births of each of her three children because she was fortunate to find stable in-home child care through personal networks. Her first nanny, a Bolivian woman, was recommended by a friend who employed a live-in domestic worker, and the Bolivian nanny remained with the family for three years. The employer subsequently hired two other child-care providers (each of them remained with the family for a period of three years) on referral from the first nanny. The second and third child-care providers were Salvadoran women. It was through such networks that most of the Central American women interviewed in Washington entered the labor market as domestic workers and child-care providers; many later shifted over to commercial cleaning companies if they preferred to acquire more benefits and stable employment.[12]

While child-care, domestic-service, and cleaning-industry jobs lured immigrant women to the Washington area after 1960, employment in the construction and restaurant industries attracted growing numbers of immigrant men. A construction boom in the Washington area persisted for years, and a *Washington Post* report (Hilzenrath 1989) noted that in 1988 "the Washington area led North American and European cities in office construction according to a survey of 49 metropolitan markets." By the mid-1980s, the typical construction worker in the Washington area was no longer a white male (as construction workers were in other cities in the United States) but was just as likely to be a member of a minority group. Although in 1986 white males constituted 83 percent of the construction labor force nationally, numerous construction-industry employers asserted in interviews that certain building trades in the Washington area were already dominated by workers of Latin American origin. The strength of Hispanic-owned businesses in the area contributed to the rapidly expanding job markets for newly arriving Latin American immigrants, with approximately three thousand Hispanic-owned businesses operating in the metropolitan area in 1989. This was the case particularly for men who sought jobs in the area's thriving construction industry, where employers of Latin American origin maintained a strong presence. Elsewhere in the nation, 10 percent of annual revenues from Hispanic-owned businesses went to construction firms, but in the Washington area the proportion was three times that figure.[13]

Less gender-segregated than the domestic-service or construction industries, the restaurant industry is another major source of employment for immigrants. The Restaurant Association of Metropolitan Washington estimated that in 1988 close to three thousand restaurants in the Washington area employed eighty thousand people full- or part-time.[14] Many restaurant owners in the Washington area claim to be immigrants themselves and are proud of the fact that they employ head chefs and managers who are also immigrants that worked their way up from starting positions as dishwashers. The industry has long been known as one of the primary sectors of employment for foreign workers, both documented and undocumented, because of the mobility it offers to workers with little formal education and limited resources. Many of Washington's restaurateurs believe that they have a higher proportion of recent undocumented immigrants on their payrolls than that found in other cities in the United States, since the level of competition between different Hispanic groups for jobs in cities such as Los Angeles makes it easier to employ documented workers there. Although comparable proportions of Central American men and women surveyed in Washington worked in the restaurant industry, men were usually favored as chefs and waiters in the more upscale restaurants because of the age-old stereotype that waiters embody a cachet superior to waitresses.

In all of these sectors where immigrants tend to concentrate, most entry-level jobs in Washington allow workers to earn well above the minimum wage. Employment counselors at local social service agencies claim that when employers call to recruit workers with legal documents, the counselors are able to bargain for higher wages for their clients since IRCA went into effect.[15] Many recent immigrants who first resided in Los Angeles, Houston, or New York eventually descended on Washington after news about the favorable job market and wage scales in that city spread. Close to half of the Central Americans surveyed in the Washington area admitted that they resided in another U.S. city before moving to Washington, D.C., and that they moved to Washington after learning about the lucrative job market there (see Table 5).

The Initial Immigrant Neighborhoods

By 1900 the avenues around Dupont Circle had filled with the imposing homes of wealthy residents, while the small Mount Pleasant district north of the Circle attracted middle-class settlers because it was situated above the city and away from its malaria-infested regions. Mount Pleasant gradually became one of the most racially mixed neighborhoods in the District as the farther suburbs lured white residents away from the downtown area. The influx of Central and South American immigrants, which began slowly in the 1950s, escalated in the 1960s, when employees of embassies from Spanish-speaking countries and international organizations (professional and domestic workers alike) made their homes in Adams Morgan and in Mount Pleasant. More and more domestic workers remained in the city after their host families left, and they encouraged family members and friends from the home countries to join them. Latin American networks (particularly for women) quickly developed alongside those of the neighborhoods' African American residents. In

Table 5   Secondary Migration: Respondents Who Lived in Interim
Locations Before Arriving in Washington, D.C. (in percent)

	Survey Sample (N=100)	Interview Sample (N=50)
Resided in other U.S. Cities	46	18
Cities in California	21	n/a
Cities in Texas	19	n/a
Other cities	6	n/a
Lived in other cities less than one year	19	n/a
Resided in other countries before U.S.	16	6
Lived in Mexico	11	5
Lived in other countries less than one year	19	n/a

1970, after the race riots that followed the assassination of Martin Luther King, 80 percent of Mount Pleasant's residents were African American. But the composition of Mount Pleasant and its newer next-door neighborhood, Adams Morgan, changed dramatically in ensuing years; young white professionals began to move into the neighborhood as renters and home owners, and immigrants from Central and South American countries converged on the area along with them.

The small Spanish-speaking population residing in Adams Morgan and Mount Pleasant eventually became beachheads for the bustling settlements of Central Americans who fled their countries in the latter part of the 1970s and in the 1980s. Initially only one Italian store in the area sold Latin American produce to the new immigrants, and one Latin American priest offered assistance (and Mass) in English and in Spanish to the newcomers. Most of the patrons were women employees of the embassies or of embassy families. Eventually grocery stores run by Latin Americans, Saturday-night dances at two area churches, and Spanish-language films at the Ontario Theatre helped to coalesce the expanding Latin American community. Puerto Rican immigrants held distinct advantages over other Latin American immigrants—most of them were already U.S. citizens who spoke English well—and in 1970 they provided the inspiration and leadership for an Office of Latino Affairs in the D.C. government. The streets of Mount Pleasant and Adams Morgan changed to such an extent that many of the African American store owners, who in the 1960s had replaced most of the founding white owners (largely Italian, Irish, and Jewish), were replaced by Latin Americans and Asians in the 1980s. While not technically immigrant enclaves, Adams Morgan and Mount Pleasant became "immigrant neighborhoods," or areas that supply residents with cultural amenities and support but not necessarily with employment opportunities.[16]

With the influx of young white professionals into the area in the 1980s, housing prices and rents in Adams Morgan and Mount Pleasant rose tremendously as both neighborhoods became gentrified—highly desirable because they had "character" and lay close to the city center. Gentrification drove many new immigrants out of the inner-city neighborhoods to less expensive suburbs in Maryland and Virginia, which in addition to lower rent had the advantage of lying closer to available jobs in outlying areas. Yet today these two inner-city neighborhoods still maintain links with the Latin American community throughout the metropolitan area by hosting annual festivals in the neighborhoods and through the numerous social service agencies based there.[17] Established by churches, local governments, and private-interest groups as the numbers of immigrants into the area surged, the social service agencies provide various services that refugees and new arrivals might require. When the initial immigrants from Central American countries first converged on the Washington area in the 1960s, there were few community agencies that had tailored programs for Spanish-speaking newcomers in order to smooth their transition to life in the United States. Today more than thirty social service agencies in the city offer immigration, educational, medical, and employment services to new immigrants. The Spanish Catholic Center alone receives fifty thousand clients each year, and over twenty parishes currently conduct Masses in Spanish. Women counselors constitute the majority on the staffs of these social service agencies, and a preponderance of them are immigrants themselves.

Rhina Garcia, for example, was a nurse from Guatemala who counseled at one agency providing pre- and postnatal services to needy women of Latin American origin. It is her ambition to respond sympathetically to the myriad dilemmas confronting clients who, without the support of extended family, must integrate themselves as wage earners and as mothers into a strange society. The day of our interview Rhina was preoccupied with an eighteen-year-old Nicaraguan mother and a toddler in the throes of a tantrum typical for her age. The mother had slapped the child to arrest the tantrum, but the child's screams continued to reverberate throughout the old Columbia Road mansion as other women pleaded with the mother in Spanish to stop. Before the distraught mother could hit the toddler again, Rhina rushed over and lifted the child to her feet. She questioned the child in a firm but soothing voice, attempting to show the teenage mother how to deal with a tantrum. But the child continued to sob while Rhina hugged her and the mother gestured and argued with a friend. Other women with children exchanged glances and one shook her head in disapproval. The sight of the child being struck several times clearly disturbed the other women.

Rhina ushered the women into a large comfortable room off the main hall, where they arranged themselves on sofas lining the walls and on floor pillows. When a cook brought hot meals to the children, seated in the cavernous dining hall, silence finally prevailed. Rhina perched on the edge of a sofa, and the women curtailed their conversations to give her full attention. She made a few announcements about afternoon English classes and about a lunchtime speaker who would discuss with them the dangers of AIDS. The women displayed obvious interest in the issue and nodded to one another. Rhina then asked the women what topic they wished to discuss that day, and one voice called out in Spanish, "How to discipline children!" The others laughed and decided that it was a good topic for the day.

Several blocks away, on 18th Street, Marina Suarez was busy later that day with a young man from El Salvador who came to her seeking employment. As the young man's counselor, Marina was also responsible for reviewing his testimony with him before he appeared at a hearing on his political asylum application the following morning. She was frequently interrupted by phone calls from other clients or from prospective employers. She indicated to the young man that he should wait, then she accepted a call from an employer who wished to advertise a handful of vacancies at his restaurant. When she put down the receiver, Marina informed her client about the kitchen positions available at the neighborhood restaurant. The young man shook his head and replied that dishwashers only earn minimum wage, whereas his former job at a demolition site paid $11 an hour. He wanted her to help him find another demolition job even though Marina warned him about the dangers of working with asbestos and expressed her concern about the obvious lack of safety standards at his former job site. Nonetheless he preferred to stand in line outside a store in Adams Morgan, at one of the well-known intersections in Washington where immigrant men wait each weekday morning for contractors and private employers to hire them for the day. He was convinced that he could earn more money that way, and he had had only one bad experience thus far with the day-labor line. He related to Marina the account of how two months earlier he had been picked up by a contractor to paint houses in a distant Maryland suburb and had worked for three days with four other men painting the interior of a newly renovated home. The contractor had refused to pay them when the job was finished, on the pretext that the work was substandard. Marina was unable to help him retrieve his wages, because he did not know the name of the employer or the exact location of the house he had painted. Marina explained that abuse of employees without legal documents was quite common and that most immigrants victimized in this way were afraid to report the incidents or to seek redress from their employers.

Uneasy Alliances in Washington's Neighborhoods

In a handful of decades Washington has outgrown its reputation as a malaria-ridden, uncultured backwater and has become known as a park-lined cosmopolitan "world city," a highly desirable domicile for young professionals and their families as well as for newcomers from other countries. But despite its wealth and an abundance of jobs, it is a city in which a great number of impoverished families struggle to survive. A third of the people living in poverty in the District of Columbia are children, four out of five are African American, and a disproportionate number (relative to their population share) are of Hispanic origin, according to a report issued in 1988.[18] A majority of people living below the poverty line cope with the high cost of housing in the Washington area by crowding together in shared spaces.[19] As apartment buildings in Adams Morgan and Mount Pleasant filled with families from Central and South American countries, many African American renters blamed them for the decline of area buildings, since Latin Americans often crowded several families into each apartment. Newly arriving refugees defined home differently from North Americans, viewing it as a sanctuary to which fellow refugees could migrate with the promise of safety and shelter.[20] Cultural differences between the two groups sometimes led to conflict in both domestic and public spaces.

Inevitably, with the massive influx of Central American immigrants willing to work for lower wages than African Americans, tensions between the two groups escalated in recent years. Despite the labor shortage that persisted throughout the Washington area for years, many African Americans perceived the newcomers as competitors for scarce resources who deflated wages for nonprofessional jobs. Immigrants from Central American countries, on the other hand, voiced the belief that African Americans were simply uninterested in working at menial jobs paying minimum wage at best. Because they were willing to do the drudge work that African Americans rejected, Central American workers claimed that they were looked upon with hostility as members of a despicable underclass.

Reality most likely lies somewhere between these stereotypic extremes and cultural differences. Among the employers interviewed for this book, most asserted that African Americans and Latin Americans form a complementary (if not always compatible) workforce. The owners of two large cleaning companies, for example, reported that a majority of their workers in District of Columbia buildings were African Americans and that workers of Latin American origin showed a greater willingness to commute to distant suburbs for cleaning jobs. Similarly, African Americans have largely abandoned the child- and elder-care businesses on their own initiative in order to move into higher-status and better-paid pink- and white-collar occupations.

But some of the construction- and landscaping-industry employers interviewed in Washington revealed a pernicious prejudice toward African American workers. A number of employers remarked that they favored Latin American workers for their eagerness, initiative, and willingness to work long hours, and a few characterized African American workers as "lazy" or "unreliable." The underlying implication may be that these employers prefer a cowed and docile immigrant workforce over African American workers, who harbor different expectations of their jobs and have a greater grasp of their rights as working citizens. U.S.-born Americans—particularly members of minority groups—understand the limitations of the labor market and may hold more sober perceptions of their positions and prospects in the labor market. Immigrants, on the other hand, and particularly those from El Salvador, are renowned among Washington-area employers for their work ethic. More recent immigrants still subscribe to the proverbial "American dream" and believe in their ability to achieve whatever success they aspire to in the United States.

Nonetheless immigrants who happen to be people of color learn the hard way what African Americans know from an early age: that dealing with discrimination and exploitation by employers or other Anglos is an intransigent North American problem. Coming from more homogeneous societies in countries such as El Salvador and Nicaragua, few Central American immigrants have experienced the depth of racial or ethnic enmity and discrimination that they encounter in the United States. Central Americans who achieved professional status and were accorded a great deal of respect in their countries of origin, for example, find that they are often denied credit by bank managers, denied jobs by employers, or refused housing by apartment managers because of their accents or appearance. Discrimination appears to be most rampant in the housing market; several of the women interviewed in Washington said that landlords refused to show them apartments once the landlords heard their Spanish accents or saw them in person. When Central Americans did find housing, landlords often failed to make repairs in their apartments or threatened to raise the rent if they did.

Washington residents of Latin American origin have also complained for years about a police force they consider abusive and on which they are vastly underrepresented. In May of 1991, pent-up tensions exploded in a melee of rioting and looting in the neighborhoods heavily populated by residents of Latin American origin: in Adams Morgan, Mount Pleasant, and Columbia Heights. The immediate incident that sparked the protests was the arrest and shooting of a Latin American man by a police officer. The officer, an African American woman, claimed that she was threatened by a man who appeared drunk and disorderly. News of the incident spread rapidly through the neighborhoods, and groups of young people, joined by ethnically diverse crowds of all ages, assembled to protest the police action. The disturbance lasted almost a week but never reached the proportions of the 1992 Los Angeles riot that followed the Rodney King verdict.[21]

In the aftermath, the D.C. Latino Civil Rights Task Force conducted a lengthy investigation into the causes of the disturbance and concluded that "the anger and frustration of the protesters was directed solely at the police. The limited episodes of looting and vandalizing businesses that occurred were subsequently determined to be mostly the acts of outside opportunists."[22] The task force charged that even though Latin American residents represented between 10 and 15 percent of Washington's population, African Americans monopolized the city government as well as city services and outreach programs. None of the city council or school board members was Spanish-speaking, and Latin Americans constituted only 1 percent of the bulging D.C. municipal workforce of forty-eight thousand. None of the fifty-nine captains on the police force was Latin American. Latino community leaders also complained that affirmative-action plans were overwhelmingly directed by African Americans for African Americans, and that Latinos did not receive a fair share of program spending and contracts. Citing "a real or perceived pattern of widespread, endemic racism and physical and verbal abuse by the Metropolitan Police Department (MPD) against the Latino Community," the task force recommended that the MPD appoint a Latino deputy police chief, recruit more Spanish-speaking officers, and develop cooperative programs to address police-community relations. Two years after the protests, the U.S. Commission on Civil Rights (1993) confirmed many of the charges leveled by Latin American community leaders. It found that "Washington's Hispanic residents were underrepresented in the city government, did not receive a fair share of city services, and were victims of abuse, harassment and misconduct by the police." The report warned that tensions could explode again in Washington and in other cities if problems affecting Hispanic Americans were not immediately addressed.

It was not within the purview of the D.C. Latino Civil Rights Task Force or the U.S. Commission on Civil Rights to address other deep-seated sources of tension between African Americans and Latin Americans. Low unemployment figures and reports about a surfeit of low-wage jobs in Washington have done little to dispel the notion among some African Americans that newcomers are robbing them of jobs and depressing wages. With the withdrawal of African Americans from certain occupational sectors (such as domestic service, child care, dishwashing, and cooking), a labor shortage in Washington persisted for almost two decades and generated jobs that drew immigrants and elevated wage levels above those in most other cities. The unemployment rate for the District of Columbia—where African Americans composed 67 percent of the population—was a low 2.9 percent in 1988 and was even lower in the surrounding suburbs. While the unemployment rate specifically for African Americans in the District of Columbia was 6.3 percent, this was relatively low in comparison with other major U.S. cities.[23] Research in various labor markets in the United States has demonstrated that the economic effects of immigration are indeed complex. Differences in regional labor markets and in sectors of the economy determine how immigrant workers are received and whether or not they compete with U.S.-born workers for jobs.[24] Some industries, regions, groups, and employees may benefit from an influx of immigrant workers, while others may suffer. Variations depend largely upon location within the United States, on the state of the local economy, and on the sector of employment or industry concerned. For example, a General Accounting Office (GAO) report stated that cleaning companies serving downtown Los Angeles replaced most of their unionized

African American workforce with nonunionized immigrants, but this has not been the case in Washington's janitorial firms. After a large-scale exodus of African Americans out of cleaning-industry jobs, those who remained tended to work primarily in the downtown Washington office buildings, whereas Latin American workers concentrated in the suburbs. In this and in other industries in the Washington area, they appeared to form a complementary workforce instead of a competitive one.

A critical element that must not be overlooked in the debate about whether immigrants compete for jobs with U.S. citizens is the gender-based features of local labor markets. The demand in the Washington labor market for child-care providers and housekeepers clearly influenced the decision-making process for many early immigrants as they cast about for employment opportunities and a destination point in the United States. Despite warnings about discrimination and other problems they would encounter in U.S. cities, Central American women in particular streamed into the Washington area upon invitation and with the promise of attractive jobs. The early pioneers discovered that they had no serious competition from Mexicans, other Latin American immigrants, or even from African Americans for certain low-wage jobs and that Washington was more livable than many other cities in North America. When larger groups of immigrants decided to flee their war-torn lands in the 1980s, they followed upon the heels of women who had established the networks and community support systems that would smooth the way for later arrivals.

Four

Labor Recruitment in the Nation's Capital

Lucia Herrera treasured her job as a housekeeper with a family from the U.S. Agency for International Development (USAID) when they were stationed in San Salvador in the late 1950s. Their home provided a refuge for the single mother, since Lucia and her daughter were then still living in her parents' crowded household. Lucia's four older brothers constantly lectured her or doled out unsolicited advice on how to raise her daughter, and she was concerned about how Maria would someday cope as a teenage girl in a "macho" household. Lucia resolved to remove her daughter from this oppressive situation because she wanted Maria to have the opportunity to choose a career and mold her own future. When Lucia's employers planned their return to Washington, they invited her to accompany them and to continue working as their housekeeper in the United States. Lucia agonized over leaving her own mother, but she accepted the offer of employment because of the limitations that her daughter would certainly confront as a young woman growing up in El Salvador. After she relocated, Lucia remained in the United States for many years, content with her life as a housekeeper in the affluent Chevy Chase section of Maryland. Her daughter, Maria, did well in the local high school there (she was one of only five foreign-born students at Bethesda–Chevy

Chase High School in 1961) and eventually went on to earn a bachelors degree at George Washington University.

Several aspects of Lucia's story are remarkable and yet typical of the outstanding qualities displayed by Central American women who chose to migrate long distances in recent decades. Lucia, like many of her compatriots of this era, was the first member of her family to journey all the way to the United States for work. Like other women from El Salvador, Guatemala, Nicaragua, and Honduras, she migrated to the Washington area under the aegis of the diplomatic family that recruited her for work. She, along with a throng of other Central American women, displayed an unusual degree of autonomy in the decision-making stages of this particular migration process. Indeed, as many as 70 percent of the Central American women interviewed in Washington claimed that they made the decision to migrate to the United States without the collaboration or assistance of partners or fathers.[1]

As previous chapters established, economic and cultural features of certain sending countries dovetailed with those of receiving cities in the United States to weight the gender ratio of the early Central American migration on the side of women. The manner in which Washington, D.C., attracted and became home to several hundred thousand Central Americans in under three decades can hardly be understood without examining the critical element of gendered labor recruitment. Lucia Herrera's and Rosa Lopez's family histories illustrate how informal labor recruitment encouraged the initial migration of Central Americans to the nation's capital.[2] Informal recruitment assumed a number of different forms. In one case, a private agency based in New York worked through contacts at the U.S. Embassy in San Salvador to recruit a woman as a domestic worker for a family living in New York in the 1960s (she and her son Manuel later moved to Washington). In other instances, diplomatic families stationed in Washington sent representatives to El Salvador and Guatemala to recruit women willing to take jobs as live-in housekeepers.

Rhina Garcia's story is typical of the latter type of recruitment, which occurred more frequently over the years. Rhina was working as a nurse in Guatemala City when she was approached by a woman and asked if she would be interested in a job in the United States. The woman was related to a diplomat employed by the World Bank whose family resided in Washington, and she was sent to search for a responsible and capable young woman who would be willing to work as a live-in nanny. Rhina had long harbored a dream to visit the United States, because for her it was "the most famous country" and she wanted to see for herself what this mecca was like. She leaped at the opportunity to live and work in Washington, even though she intended to stay only one or two years before returning to Guatemala with her accumulated savings. The year was 1977 and Rhina was the first member of her large family of nine siblings to migrate to the United States.

The recruiting relative of the World Bank family bought Rhina's plane ticket and escorted her to Washington. Rhina lived with the family in their palatial home on Foxhall Road (one of Washington's exclusive addresses) but she lasted only three months as their housekeeper. The family paid her very little ($200 a month) and asked her to work many evenings and weekends, conditions that prompted her to search for better terms of service with another family. Rhina answered a newspaper ad placed by an American family and was hired as their live-in housekeeper at twice the salary she had been earning with the diplomatic family. She remained with the American family for six months, but once again was dissatisfied with her employers' treatment. Although these two negative work experiences in the United States discouraged her, she did not want to return to Guatemala at the end of one year without having accumulated any savings. She decided to make one more effort at finding palatable employment because, as she said, "I am not a quitter!"

While sitting on a bus one day, she learned through word of mouth about a German family in Washington that was looking for a housekeeper. She interviewed for the position, secured the job, and remained with the family for three years, earning $500 per month. Ten years later she was still living and working in Washington, having acquired her permanent residency and (later) a husband. When asked if any relatives had joined her in that city over the last decade, she laughed and listed two brothers, two sisters, both parents, several cousins, and many friends from her home town. She explained that her brother had followed her to the Washington area, established a remodeling company in northern Virginia, and then offered jobs to many people from the family's home town who wanted to come to the United States for work.

In most of these cases, women were part of the initial influx of Central American immigrants to the Washington area in the 1960s and 1970s. In numerous other households women came after 1980 when relatives living in Washington arranged positions for them as live-in housekeepers with professional Washington families. Three women migrated to Washington after their sisters (who were already working in that city) were asked by diplomats stationed there to contact prospective immigrant employees. Occasionally, a friend or family member approached an employer to inquire about a job on behalf of someone who wished to immigrate to the United States.

Several men also asserted that they went to Washington because they were recruited for jobs. Twenty years ago a friend of Antonio Diego from the same town in El Salvador wrote to him from Washington and informed him of a job opening in a jewelry store in Silver Spring, Maryland. Antonio now owns his own jewelry store in the Maryland suburb, and he was responsible for bringing his brother and his brother's entire family to Washington. Another man, when offered a job at the Organization of American States, brought along in succession his wife, two children, and two housekeepers (who eventually imported their families as well) from El Salvador. Two men migrated to Washington to work in the construction industry after friends sent them job contracts that they had arranged with employers of Latin

American origin. Others came at the invitation of a sibling, parent, uncle, or aunt and found work soon afterward with the assistance of relatives.

Women Pioneer the Way to Washington

Central American migration patterns were heavily influenced by structural features that distinguish Washington from other major urban centers in the United States. As the center of national government and headquarters for many international agencies, Washington hosts approximately 131 embassies or lower-level diplomatic missions, which bring over twenty thousand staff and families to the city. Several thousand other foreign-born residents work for international businesses and organizations (such as the World Bank and International Monetary Fund), and they import staff and service workers as well. The area's six major universities attract nearly ten thousand foreign students annually, bringing the total of foreign-born professional workers, students, and private staff to around fifty thousand in any given year.[3] Thus the nation's capital has rapidly become home to a burgeoning community of foreign-born residents, professional and household workers alike, who stayed on after their tenure of employment was finished.

The extent to which foreign-born professionals—along with diplomatic families and employees of U.S. government agencies—instigated the convergence upon Washington of service workers from other countries becomes clear in the figures from this and other Washington-based studies. Among both of my samples of Central Americans in Washington, 70 percent of those who moved to the nation's capital before 1980 were women. This affirms the findings of Lucy Cohen's 1980 study, that 69 percent of Central and South American immigrants to the Washington area in the 1960s and 1970s were women (see Table 6).[4] Linda Martin and Kerry Segrave (1985) observed elsewhere that nearly half of the 120,000 U.S. visas granted to Latin

Table 6   Sex of Respondents by Date of Migration toWashington (in percent)

	Survey Sample (N=100)	Interview Sample (N=50)
Women respondents	43	66
Men respondents	57	34
Pre-1980 immigrants out of total	14	26
Proportion of pre-1980 immigrants who were women	71	69
Proportion of pre-1980 immigrants who were men	29	31
1980s immigrants out of total	86	74
Proportion of 1980 immigrants who were women	38	62
Proportion of 1980 immigrants who were men	62	38

American women in 1968 were for prospective live-in domestic workers.[5]

Nearly one-third of the pre-1980 immigrants interviewed in Washington and a fifth of those surveyed were recruited by employers directly or through other Central Americans who were already working in that city (see Table 7). However, a large percentage of the survey respondents were not the first members of their families to migrate to the United States, and most of them arrived in the Washington area after 1980. Among the relatives of respondents who were the first persons to migrate to the Washington area (primarily before the 1980s), a far larger percentage of them were women who had jobs arranged or who were recruited to work in that city. The hypothesis that many of the early Central American immigrants were women who were recruited to work or had jobs arranged for them proved to be

Table 7   Reasons Respondents Gave for Choosing to Live in
Washington, D.C. (in percent)

	Pre-1980s Migrants (N=27)	1980s Migrants (N=123)
Recruited to work or	21(A)	20(A)
had job arranged	33(B)	5(B)
Relative(s) in D.C.	50(A)	48(A)
	38(B)	68(B)
Heard there were more jobs	21(A)	26(A)
or higher wages in D.C.	31(B)	19(B)
Miscellaneous reasons	8(A)	6(A)
	0(B)	8(B)

Note: A is an abbreviation for the survey sample, and B represents the interview sample.

valid particularly for the original immigrant from each respondent's family who moved to the Washington area. Among the original pre-1980 immigrants in each respondent's family, fully 70 percent from the survey sample (50 percent from the interview sample) were recruited to work or had jobs arranged for them in Washington (see Table 8). The comparable figure for later immigrants (those who came in the 1980s) was around 20 percent (25 percent for the interview sample).[6]

Rosa Lopez's family history exemplifies the extent to which recruitment and gender-based social networks operated as determining factors in both the decision to migrate and the eventual choice of destination. Rosa (who was introduced in Chapter One) had been working in San Salvador for a USAID family that eventually invited her to return with them to Washington and

Table 8   Reasons Original Immigrants in Respondents' Families
Chose to Live in Washington, D.C. (in percent)

	Survey Sample (N=100)	Interview Sample (N=50)	Pre-1980s (N=27)	1980 (N=123)
Original immigrant arrived in D.C. before 1980*	43	67	—	—
Original immigrant to D.C. were women**	52	58	71(A) 70(B)	36(A) 67(B)
Original immigrant had job arranged or was recruited to work in D.C.***	43	36	70(A) 45(B)	20(A) 25(B)
Original immigrant heard there were more jobs or higher wages in D.C.	34	49	10(A) 50(B)	57(A) 50(B)
Original immigrant had friends in D.C.	16	9	10(A) 0(B)	16(A) 25(B)
Miscellaneous reasons	7	6	10(A) 5(B)	6(A) 17(B)

Note: A is an abbreviation for the survey sample, and B represents the interview sample.

* These are the percentages of respondents who knew when the original immigrants in their families went to Washington, D.C.

** These are the percentages of respondents who knew the identities (whether men or women) of the original immigrants in their families who went to Washington.

*** These are the percentages of respondents who knew the identities of the original immigrants in their families, when they arrived in Washington, and their reasons for choosing to live in that city.

work as their housekeeper. In the 1970s Rosa and her husband invited several nieces to join them, and they in turn made it possible for other women in the family to find work in Washington. Rosa arranged a position for Teresa (one of her husband's nieces) as a live-in housekeeper for a diplomatic family in Washington. Several years later, Teresa learned that her cousin Eva had been unemployed for almost two years, since the government had closed the university in San Salvador, and that Eva was afraid to go out at night because of the violence in the city. She sent Eva the money for a visa and a plane ticket to Washington and helped her cousin find day-time housecleaning positions through her own employers. Meanwhile Rosa arranged a live-in child-care position with a diplomatic family for another niece (Carmen). Over time, thirty-five members of this large extended family have gravitated to the Washington area. The women as well as their partners found jobs primarily through other women's networks. In this and in other families, women formed their own networks for securing employment and for recruiting others in their job searches, since they outnumbered men among early arrivals in the city before community agencies or support systems for Latin American newcomers existed.

In concordance with the "chain migration" literature, many of the later immigrants from Central American countries (50 percent) said that they chose to go to Washington because they already had a family member living in the area. A significant number also claimed they had heard that there were more jobs and higher wages in Washington than in other U.S. cities. Isabel Martinez was one of the women who learned about the job market in Washington after she left El Salvador to escape an abusive partner. She explained:

> I came to the United States in 1975 and I was in Los Angeles for one year and a half. I worked for six months in a house, living in, and about one year in a dry cleaners, ironing. I liked it in Los Angeles, but when my brother came, he said we should go to Wash-

ington because in Washington we could get better jobs. Some people told him that. So we came to Washington and I got a job as a dishwasher. I had all kinds of jobs here. Now I am a receptionist and I like my job very much.

Several other women, including Anna Fernandez, said that before they even left their countries of origin, they knew it was harder to get jobs in Los Angeles and New York than in Washington. Anna had been abandoned by her partner and became the sole person responsible for the support of her mother and her small daughter. Her job in Guatemala City did not pay well and Anna's partner refused to provide her any child support, so Anna decided to try her luck in the United States and from there send money home to her mother and daughter. She learned about a Mexican woman who sold jewelry in El Salvador and Guatemala and who drove people across the border into the United States for a small fee ($400). This woman even offered her clients a place to stay when they first arrived in a city, and she agreed to arrange living space for Anna in Los Angeles. But after one week in that city Anna decided to head directly for Washington, D.C., because a friend from Guatemala who was already living there wrote and told her that she could secure a job that paid high wages. The Mexican woman gave Anna the name of a contact with whom she could stay in Wheaton, Maryland; the woman in Wheaton subsequently provided Anna with a temporary room, until she could find a place of her own, and even employed Anna to help clean apartments in the building.

Another woman joined her uncle (Manuel) in Washington to attend university there. Manuel and his mother had migrated to New York years before, when she was recruited to work as a housekeeper for a family in that city. After working for several years in the shipyards of New York, Manuel went to Washington because he heard that in the Washington area there was less competition with other Latin Americans for jobs. A few Central American immigrants in my study chose Washington as their destination because they had been encouraged to do so (sometimes with offers of jobs) by friends who had moved there. Two students chose to go to colleges in the Washington area, and an elderly woman went to join her daughter in that city when the woman became ill. Several others felt that the nation's capital must be the most important city in the country and therefore the best place to make money. Two women from El Salvador asserted that living in Washington was their fondest dream and that they had felt isolated in the smaller U.S. cities where they had first resided. These informants believed that people in Washington were more tolerant of foreigners and more familiar with other cultures and countries. Finally, Washington's distance from the U.S.-Mexican border provided an added attraction, since cities in California and Texas were considered by some to be less safe than those in the Northeast because of the concentration of INS personnel in the Southwest. Other informants felt that in Los Angeles and in Houston the turf was already taken (primarily by Mexican immigrants or by other Central Americans) and that in the Northeast there was less competition for jobs and housing.

Networks eventually operated at such a pitch that from several Salvadoran towns, entire communities and families trailed into the U.S. capital after the initial pioneers. The town of Intipuca in El Salvador, for example, sent so many immigrants to the Washington, D.C., area that the town grew affluent from the high rate of remissions sent from Washington immigrants to relatives back home (the town even renamed one of its major avenues Washington Street). Half the population of another Salvadoran town, Chirilagua, currently resides in a northern Virginia suburb. Original immigrants—many of whom were recruited to work—established themselves to the extent that they could invite friends and family to join them as networks hummed with news about the favorable job market and wage levels in Washington.

The Idiosyncracies of a Gendered Migration

The most striking revelation to emerge from interviews with Central American immigrants in the Washington area was the inordinate number of women who made the decision to migrate on their own, without the collaboration or assistance of male partners, fathers, or brothers. Over two-thirds of the women interviewed declared that they did not follow or accompany a male partner, but instead journeyed to the United States on their own volition—sometimes accompanied by children. Some of the women had experienced circumstances similar to Isabel Martinez, who fled her province in El Salvador in order to escape an abusive partner. Others, like Lucia Herrera, had been abandoned by husbands or partners and realized that they could not provide for themselves or their children as single mothers in their countries of origin. Rhina Garcia is typical of the many single women who simply seized the opportunity to fashion more lucrative and challenging careers for themselves, particularly when presented with the offer of employment in the United States.

Half the women who made the decision to migrate on their own or with children did so for reasons related to civil war. Several teachers attested that they were persecuted for comments or inferences reported by students in their classrooms. Even more women declared that they feared for the lives of sons or daughters; one older mother saw her house burned, her bakery business destroyed, and one son grazed by a bullet before she fled Morazan Province (in El Salvador) with her children. Others, like Julia Mendez, experienced torture and persecution firsthand. Julia was desperate to leave El Salvador in 1986 after she was assaulted twice in her province of San Miguel by men who were dressed like soldiers. She also received two anonymous letters carrying death threats. Julia's cousin, who had worked for three years for a Salvadoran family living in Washington, D.C., returned from that city to San Salvador and gave Julia the address of her former employers, who were diplomats working for

the Inter-American Development Bank. Julia took it upon herself to travel to the U.S. capital alone—first by bus, then by foot
across the border, then by bus once again. She contacted the family her cousin had worked for as soon as she arrived in Washington, and they agreed to take her on as their live-in housekeeper.

This revelation, that many Central American women exhibited the autonomy and gumption to migrate long distances on
their own, stands in sharp contrast to the mainstream literature
on gender and migration patterns. Indeed, women's roles in the
decision-making stage before migration occurs has only recently
emerged as a subject worthy of attention. Earlier research was
guided by the assumption that women passively follow econom-
ically motivated males to the United States, and even recent studies insinuate that women generally migrate to create or reunite
families. Studies of Mexican immigrants to the United States, for
example, point out that circular flows of mostly undocumented
"lone male" short-stay migrants, working primarily in seasonal
agricultural, once characterized Mexican migration patterns to
the United States. This pattern shifted in the 1980s, when Mexican migration became more heterogeneous and more women
began to migrate to California because of employment opportunities as domestic workers, baby-sitters, and laundry workers—
jobs that are stereotypically reserved for women (and particularly for women of color).[7] A recent study on family stage
migration among Mexicans residing in California found that
husbands generally decided to migrate with only token regard
for their wives' opinions. Similarly, men from the Dominican Republic generally migrated to the United States for work after fathers in patrilateral extended households decided which sons
should emigrate. Wives who agreed to join their husbands usually did so because the Dominican immigrant community in the
United States offered little resistance to women working outside
the household for wages. In effect, migration was a means by
which Dominican women, once they obtained paid employment

in the United States, could escape total dependence on their husbands.[8]

Unlike the Mexican and Dominican women in these studies, Central American women displayed an unusual degree of autonomy in their decisions to migrate with inducements similar to those that drew immigrant men to other parts of the United States. Twenty-two of the thirty women interviewed in Washington said that they did not follow or accompany a male partner when they moved to the United States, but migrated on their own or brought a child or children along. Only six of the thirty women were married or accompanied male partners at the time of their migration, and two others accompanied fathers. Nearly half of the women were single and migrated to the United States alone, and ten women were single mothers who were divorced or abandoned by their partners. Most of the women who migrated on their own and without men shared two key characteristics: they migrated directly from the capital cities in their countries of origin and had moderate to high levels of education—only two had completed as few as six years in school, and six held college degrees.

A number of employers in the Washington area implied that they intentionally recruited Central (and South) American women when they were seeking housekeepers and child-care providers. Some of these employers voiced the opinion that Central American women were more diligent, reliable, and willing to work hard in low-wage occupations than were North Americans. It may be that an element of "positive typification" surrounds Central American workers, since several private employers of Central American nannies expressed the belief that these women were very warm and nurturing with children. The work ethic for which Salvadorans in particular are renowned applies to women as well as to men, since women have participated in the wage-labor force for decades. Two employers emphasized that they wished to expose their children to another language and culture and therefore sought out Spanish-speaking child-care providers—an attitude that might be more prevalent in Washington than elsewhere in the country. The proximity of the Central American countries to the United States also facilitated the recruitment of these workers because transportation and other costs were less than the costs of recruiting immigrant workers from more distant points.

For Central American job seekers, increasing economic and cultural ties between the United States and the Central American countries since 1960 (via media, social networks, factories, and other job sites) also made the distances and differences between the regions less formidable. In countries with low marriage rates such as El Salvador, women were at liberty to migrate longer distances without the encumbrances of family responsibilities. News of the availability of an ample and eager low-wage workforce spread rapidly among professional families in the nation's capital, where U.S.-born workers were no longer available or willing to perform poorly paid and low-status work in domestic service. The fundamental motive for recruiting Central American women into domestic-service and child-care positions remained the scarcity of alternative labor sources. Since the 1960s African American women as well as Anglo women voted with their feet and retreated in large numbers from domestic service, the most poorly paid and low-status employment sector in the United States. When employers scanned the market for eligible household help and child-care providers, they found almost exclusively women of color from third-world countries who had few options for more lucrative employment. In recent decades Latinas have come to constitute the largest category of women entering domestic service, as Mary Romero has observed elsewhere (1992:71).

Gender proved to be a critical element in both the decision to migrate as well as the reluctance to return to the country of origin. Studies of Mexican immigrants in California as well as Jamaicans and Dominicans in New York found that nearly all women preferred permanent settlement in the United States in opposition to men's desire for return migration. Ostensibly, women wished to maintain the gains they had won with migration and employment in the United States.[9] Five years after the initial interviews with thirty Central American women in Washington, I was able to locate two-thirds of the respondents in the interview sample, and only two of them had returned to their country of origin. For reasons noted earlier, few Central American men and women in Washington engage in a gender-based struggle over the issue of return migration. Given the high incidence of female-headed households in countries such as El Salvador and Guatemala, Central American women's participation in the wage-labor force was hardly a novelty. Many of the women migrated to the United States as single women or single mothers specifically to improve their occupational positions or earnings, and few couples engaged in debates about whether women should work in the United States. Because of the continuing civil strife in their countries of origin, Central American men and women appeared to be in agreement that the circumstances for return migration were less than optimal, particularly for their children.

The Consequences of Gendered Migrations

The most distinctive consequence of the gendered migration pattern that Central Americans moving to Washington established is that it appeared to result in more permanent immigration and settlement than those led by men. Notable gender differences emerged in settlement patterns among Central American women and men early on, as women who were recruited to work in Washington brought more family members along with them or sent for them sooner than recruited men did. All of the women who went to Washington with job offers claimed that they arrived in the United States with legal documents; most of them had attained permanent-resident status by the time of the interviews; and they brought or sent for family members soon after their arrival. The relatives they brought with them also tended to migrate legally, to find jobs quickly through the initial immigrant's network, and to become permanent residents. On the other hand, only 20 percent of the men who had jobs arranged for them in Washington (compared with 87 percent for the women in this category) brought family members along or sent for them soon after migration. Half of the men admitted that they held no work permits or only temporary work permits after applying for political asylum.

The discrepancy between the documented status for the women who went to Washington with job offers and the undocumented status for men is due in part to the earlier migration of women (more of the men went to Washington in the 1980s). It may also reflect the preponderance of women among domestic workers; since these workers had opportunities to develop close bonds with the families for whom they worked, the families in turn were more inclined to sponsor the women for labor certification. In contrast, several men complained that their employers (primarily those in the construction industry) had not been forthcoming in helping them to apply for legal status—even if they had been promised such assistance before they accepted a job. The discrepancy might also reflect a greater proclivity on the part of women to maintain close ties with relatives in their home countries and to help them emigrate sooner than men did.

Thomas Kessner's 1977 study of Italian migration to the United States in the early 1900s expounded on the more common migration pattern in which men outnumber women, noting that these migrations usually resulted in temporary settlement, the sending of large remittances back home, and a great deal of return migration. Conversely, Hasia Diner's 1983 study of Irish immigration to the United States in the nineteenth century observed the following consequences of a migration in which women predominated over men: women concentrated in domestic service because they were single and able to live in; they accumulated savings rapidly; they brought over numerous relatives (especially other women), which resulted in more permanent immigration; and they were able to finance their own upward mobility into nursing or stenography, which led to a more thorough "Americanization."[10] Some of these same advantages accrued to Central American women who pioneered the movement to cities in the United States. Like the Irish women above, Central American women used their savings to support families and children back home, to bring relatives to the United States, and to acquire consumer goods (such as cars, televisions, even home mortgages). As in the earlier Irish migration, Central American women tended to concentrate in domestic-service jobs upon arrival, and they immediately sent for other relatives (primarily women), who also opted for permanent settlement in the United States.

However, the recent migration of Central Americans to the United States differs from other migrations in which women predominated in several fundamental aspects. Civil war provided incentive and urgency to many Central Americans who fled for their personal safety or that of their children. Many Central American single mothers emigrated in order to support children and families they left back home or brought with them to the United States. Family encumbrances and demands for assistance from those left behind in countries of origin often consumed whatever income women would otherwise have safeguarded to finance their own education and upward mobility. There is little evidence thus far to suggest that savings has allowed them to finance their own upward mobility, since Central American women have not evinced higher rates of social mobility than Central American men (as Irish women did long ago). The salient difference is that women of color face a more obstructed career trajectory than did Irish women, who were able with time to progress to nursing, secretarial, or teaching jobs in the United States. Given greater language and cultural differences between theirs and the host society, Central American women must surmount considerable barriers if they aspire to leave domestic service for higher status or better-paying occupations over time.

Several authors have painstakingly demonstrated that domestic service is hardly the occupation of choice that immigrant women freely elect to enter, nor is it the "bridging occupation" to higher-status jobs for women of color that it once was considered to be for white women. Rather, it is one of the few occupations open to immigrant women, since the labor market allocates certain jobs to people by gender, color, and class, reserving low-status and poorly paid jobs for women in general and for women of color in particular.[11] Recent studies show that a disproportionate number of domestic workers are women of color and that immigrant women of color in particular are locked into domestic-service jobs without the array of opportunities for employment mobility that white women have. Romero's study, for example, demonstrated that native-born white women employed in domestic service were more likely to be treated as "help" and to obtain more favorable working conditions than were their Chicana counterparts. She points out that discriminatory institutional practices have long relegated women of color to the lowest-status and lowest-paying jobs in society; even the educational systems in some states reinforce this segregation in the labor force by channeling African American and Chicana students into vocational training courses (especially in home economics) and toward work in domestic service.

Although Central American women in Washington were favored in the recruitment efforts to fill jobs that are stereotypically defined as "women's work," they find themselves stymied in low-status occupations that are poorly paid by U.S. labor market standards. Evidence presented in the following chapter supports the assertion that women of color experience domestic service as an "occupational ghetto" rather than as a bridging occupation or transitional career on the path to upward social mobility.[12] As migration patterns of other groups (such as that of Mexicans to California) shift, and as the proportion of immigrant women among newcomers to the United States grows, the career trajectories exhibited by their Central American sisters in Washington may portend employment prospects for immigrant women in other cities in the United States.

Five

Working Women and Men in Washington's Labor Market

Early on in their sojourn in the United States, Central American women are forced to come to grips with the realization that they will confront more obstructions in the labor market than their husbands, brothers, and partners do. The vignette related earlier about Marina Suarez, the social service agency counselor who earns half what her brother does, in spite of having six more years of education and a college degree, hinted at the gaping disparity in working conditions, wage scales, and employment options for women versus men in U.S. labor markets. Marina's career trajectory and those of other Central American workers profiled here reveal many layers of differences between immigrant men and women in their labor market insertion patterns, leverage in negotiating wages and work conditions, and employment mobility in the United States. As the Central American migration process evolved from an employer-induced to a family-based migration, the women who forged ahead to the Washington area eventually found their wages lagging far behind male compatriots who arrived after them.

Debates about why some immigrants fare better than others in U.S. labor markets generally revolve around whether personal background characteristics or structural factors (e.g., the sector of the economy in which they work) determine how much immigrants earn and how much occupational mobility they may expect. Human capital theory posits that personal characteristics of immigrants—that is, education and skill level, work experience and general social skills—account for most income differences. If this were the case then immigrants' earnings should increase with U.S. labor market experience, higher levels of education, and English-speaking ability.[1] Historical-structural theory challenges the supposition that with sufficient time in the United States immigrants will eventually fare as well as native-born groups and that individual characteristics of immigrants are the main determinants of earnings.[2] It predicts that the structure of the labor market and the sector in which immigrants work will have greater impact on wages and that income differences will persist despite the influence of individual skills and traits. Workers in the primary labor market (i.e., those who work in larger mainstream or multinational companies) should receive higher wages than those in the secondary market (generally associated with smaller private businesses).

While voluminous research has focused on the economic performance of immigrant men, few studies have thoughtfully assessed women's labor market experiences or compared the earnings of immigrant women with those of immigrant men. One study found that education level had the greatest influence on occupational status for Hispanic women, followed by structural characteristics such as the sector of employment and ethnic composition of the labor market. The data and life histories related in this book reinforce the importance of highlighting gender factors in the labor market performance of immigrants, especially in the protracted debate over immigrant economic success. Gender is as critical as structural or personal characteristics in determining how immigrants are incorporated into U.S. labor markets and how well they perform over time. The stories of Rhina Garcia and of Rosa Lopez and her various family members illustrate how gender factors in conjunction with structural barriers in the labor market pose obstacles to women's occupational success and render them incapable of fully capitalizing on their personal (human capital) advantages.

Rhina Garcia was the young Guatemalan nurse introduced in Chapter Three who resigned herself to lower-status work as a housekeeper for a diplomatic family in order to have the opportunity to live and work in the United States. After surviving two short but unpleasant experiences caring for the children of professional Washington families, she made one final attempt to locate acceptable employment. With a third foray into the realm of live-in domestic workers, Rhina was satisfied with her German employers, who paid her $6,000 per annum—twice what the first family had paid—and she remained with the family for three years. But Rhina was ambitious, intelligent, and in possession of a bachelor's degree in nursing, and she enrolled in English-language classes at a local school to improve her marketability. Then she learned that cleaning positions were available at one of Washington's downtown hotels and made the leap from live-in to day work in domestic service. The job paid her a salary of $12,500 (in 1980), and with that Rhina finally could afford to move into an apartment of her own. She worked in that capacity for three years until she had saved enough money to enroll in culinary school. After several years' work as a caterer, she qualified as a permanent resident and married a fellow Guatemalan. When a friend told her about a counseling position that was available at a social service agency that provided pre- and postnatal services to women from Latin American countries, Rhina applied for the position and won it. After working at the agency for two years, she still earned $14,500 (about $7 an hour), only slightly more than what she had been earning as a housekeeper at a hotel eight years earlier and far from adequate if she was ever to realize her dream of buying a home with her new husband. But she elicited great enthusiasm for her job because of the challenges involved, the higher status it carried, and the fulfillment she received from it. "I love babies and I love working with my own people," she explained. "I understand these women so well and I want them to be able to do something better than cleaning houses."

Shortly after Rosa Lopez followed the USAID family for whom she had worked in San Salvador to Washington, she summoned the first of several nieces to a full-time position as a live-in housekeeper for a diplomatic couple in Washington. The Spanish-speaking diplomats paid Teresa only $60 a month plus room and board (the equivalent of 38¢ an hour) to look after five children. She lasted one year on this job, then found a similar position (working for other Spanish-speaking diplomats). It paid $75 a month, so after another year she sought better wages. The next housekeeping job she secured paid $200 a month, and she remained with the diplomatic family (also from a Latin American country) for three years. When she moved on to become a nanny for a fourth family, her salary jumped to $480 per month. After eight years of live-in work, during which she resided in other people's houses, Teresa moved into an apartment of her own. Through a friend she found daytime house-cleaning jobs that paid $35 per day. Ten years later she was earning $50 per day for a six-hour work day (about $8 per hour), which left her afternoons free and allowed her to be home in time to meet her son after school. She spoke fluent English, had obtained permanent residency, and lived with a companion who had emigrated from Honduras only three years before. Although she knew that she would never be able to do any other type of work, given her limited education (three years of schooling), she was nonetheless content with her accomplishments in the United States: she had her own car and apartment and as a single mother had provided well for her son.

In the late 1970s Rosa sent money for passage and a visa to a second niece, Rosaria, after arranging a job for her as a live-in housekeeper for an Argentinian diplomat's family. Rosaria worked for the Argentinian family for two years at $80 per month plus room and board—the equivalent of 50¢ an hour. With nine years of education and several years of experience working in a clothing factory in El Salvador, she was ill prepared for any other work in the Washington area besides housekeeping or childcare. She moved into an apartment when her fiancé from El Salvador arrived, and after they married she accepted various daytime housecleaning jobs arranged through her cousin Teresa's network. She cleaned houses for $40 a day (about $6 per hour) for four years before she was able to find a position more to her liking as a dressmaker in a clothing store, at which she earned only $5 an hour. With such low wages she was forced to supplement her earnings with weekend cleaning jobs. Her husband Manuel (who also had nine years of education upon his arrival in the United States) worked for four years at a Latin American grocery store in Adams Morgan. He earned only $4 per hour during those years, but the grocery store owner eventually sponsored him and helped him attain permanent residency. Subsequently, he secured a job as a carpenter at a large construction company and earned $14 per hour until recession stalled the Washington area's construction frenzy. Manuel was laid off in 1991 and Rosaria was forced to support the family by working two full-time jobs.

Jose Sandoval, a young amnesty applicant from El Salvador, did not always have the security of a high-paying job as he did at the time of our interview. For the first five months that he resided in Washington, Jose worked at a restaurant on Capitol Hill as a busboy, making only $3 an hour. A friend told him about a small construction company in northern Virginia that needed painters, and Jose eagerly switched occupations. While working as a painter he learned the drywall-finishing and plastering business as well, and by the end of his five years with the company he was earning $10 an hour. Then he read in a newspaper ad that Raul DeVargas's company was looking for drywall finishers, and he applied for a position. His starting wage was $14 an hour. Two years later, when he ran afoul of DeVargas over the issue of his brother's legal documents, he quit the company and found a job immediately with another large (American-owned) construction company in Virginia. Because he had to commute one hour each way to work, he negotiated his wages up to $16 an hour. When his employer asked if he knew of anyone else who was looking for work, he brought one of his brothers into the company. The employer offered his brother $14 an hour, but Jose bargained them up to $15. Meanwhile his wife Luisa, who has two more years of education than Jose, had been cleaning houses for seven years at $45 per house (about $7 an hour). Jose lamented the fact that life in the United States was not particularly satisfying for immigrants, because "we always have to work very hard and scrimp and save and never have enough money." He added, "Even if I can save $100,000, what is $100,000 in this country? You can't relax, you still have to work hard." He therefore planned to save as much money as possible over the next few years and then relocate to Costa Rica or Guatemala, where he and his wife would be able to purchase a small business and a house.

The experiences of the women and men recounted above hint at gender's greater influence, compared with that of either structural or personal background characteristics, in determining how immigrants fare in certain labor markets in the United States. The three women described here earned roughly equal salaries after years of experience in various sectors of the U.S. labor market despite the fact that Rhina Garcia was a college graduate, Rosaria Lopez had nine years of education, and Teresa Lopez had three. Jose Sandoval, on the other hand, only finished sixth grade, and he earned almost twice what any of the women earned. And yet these low-earning women had more job security and were able to retain their jobs when recession set in, unlike several high-earning men who worked in the construction industry.

In this chapter, gender figures prominently in the analysis of several key issues in the study of international labor migrations.

The first section charts the trends and peculiarities of Central American women's and men's labor market insertion patterns in the Washington metropolitan area. The second section offers an analysis of the influence of structural versus human capital variables on wage levels and occupational mobility in order to assess immigrant economic performance in this particular labor market. A final section reveals the ways in which the experiences of Central American women and men in Washington's labor market constitute new immigration patterns atypical of the trajectories followed by earlier immigrant groups.

Labor Market Insertion Patterns

In the 1980s Central American men journeyed all the way to Washington—often from cities in Texas and California—with advance knowledge that the nation's capital offered higher-paying jobs and less competition with other Latin American workers than other U.S. cities did. News about the construction boom in Washington and about the ease with which Spanish-speaking men, whether documented or undocumented, could secure employment influenced some of the Central American men in their decision to leave their countries of origin in the first place. Jose Sandoval, for one, recalls that in 1979 a close friend of his older brother returned to Chalatenango (in El Salvador) after working for two years in Washington, D.C. The friend regaled Jose and his brother with stories about the abundance of jobs, favorable working conditions, and high wages in the U.S. capital, and he persuaded his friends to join him upon his return to the United States. Another Salvadoran man claimed that for the three years preceding our interview he had resided with his wife in Los Angeles during the winter months and had journeyed to Washington every spring when the building season commenced. He worked for an Argentinian man who owned a mid-size construction firm, and asserted that his wages in Washington were higher than what he could earn in Los Angeles.

The primary reason that Central American men gravitate toward work in Washington's construction industry is that wages in construction are higher than almost any other sector in which international migrants labor. Also, construction jobs were plentiful in the Washington area throughout the 1980s and there was little competition with immigrants from other Latin American countries for such jobs. While African American men maintained their predominance in certain sectors (such as skilled trades) within the construction industry in Washington, Central American men swelled the ranks of painters, laborers, and landscapers throughout the 1980s.[3] Among the Central American men surveyed in Washington, 61 percent were working in construction at the time of the surveys, 18 percent were employed in the restaurant industry, and 7 percent worked for cleaning companies.[4] These three industries alone accounted for 88 percent of the jobs for men, and the unemployment rate for survey participants was under 3 percent (see Table 9).

Labor market insertion patterns for Central American men parallel those for women to the extent that most men claimed to have located jobs through social networks. Among earlier immigrants the men allege that a cousin, brother, sister, or friend recruited or enticed them to the Washington area with promises of assistance in securing employment. Like the women from their countries of origin, men often received on-the-job training as well as assistance from compatriots in negotiating wages or work conditions. Jose Sandoval, for example, began his career with a stint in a small construction firm owned by a man of Latin American origin. Jose had never handled a paint brush, so his partners taught him the trade and, in time, drywall and plaster work as well. Eventually, after he became a competent drywall finisher, he was able to negotiate his own wages and those of his brother.

Because domestic service was always available, it also provided strong incentive for women facing the decision whether to emigrate from their countries of origin. Numerous studies found

Table 9 Current Employment Categories and Wages for Men

Current Job	Survey Sample			Interview Sample		
	N	%	Median Wages	N	%	Median Wages
Total construction	35	(61)	$9.18	9	(53)	$10.63
Skilled workers	13	(23)		3	(18)	15.00
Semiskilled	3	(5)		0		
Laborers	11	(19)		3	(18)	7.50
Painters	8	(14)		3	(18)	10.38
Landscaping	4	(7)	6.30	0		
Total restaurant	10	(18)	6.25	4	(24)	6.65
Hotel/banquet	0			2	(12)	7.50
Waiters	0			1	(6)	7.50
Busboys	4	(7)		1	(6)	4.00
Dishwashers	2	(4)		0		
Cooks	4	(7)		0		
Cleaning/maint.	4	(7)	5.78	0		
Other:	2	(4)	6.25	4	(24)	7.00
Accountant	0			1	(6)	7.50
Business/retail	2	(4)		0		
Engineer	0			1	(6)	
Factory	0			1	(6)	7.00
Pool Cleaning	0			1	(6)	6.50
Unemployed	1	(2)				
Sporadic work	1	(2)				

Note: Hourly wages are calculated on the basis of a 40-hour work week. The range for men's wages in the survey of 100 households was $4.18 to $14.00; the range for those in the interview sample was $4.00 to $18.00.

this to be the case for women within Latin American countries who moved from rural to urban areas, and it applies as well to Central American women who chose to migrate to the United States.[5] Most of the women interviewed in Washington who left their countries of origin before 1980 said that they knew domestic service was an option for them in the United States and that they had heard about the surfeit of such jobs in the Washington area. Almost half of the women who emigrated before 1980 were actually recruited to work or had jobs arranged for them in domestic service in the Washington area. Many of the women who migrated after 1980 and who spoke of violence and political persecution as primary motivations for leaving their countries of origin also knew that they would be able to find work in domestic service in the United States.

But there the similarities between women's and men's labor market insertion patterns end. While Central American women located employment or might have been recruited in the same way as men—through employers or gender-based social networks—their work conditions and leverage differed markedly from men's. Irrespective of their education levels and prior work experience, most women commenced their employment careers in the United States in domestic service—a low-status occupation that pigeonholes immigrant women to a degree unparalleled in men's occupational sectors (see Table 10, pp. 104–5). The very nature of the job performed by domestic workers carries a stigma as "degrading" work, since it involves cleaning other people's bathrooms and kitchens and picking up after employers' families. Such work is still undervalued and poorly remunerated in the labor market, and few women derive assurances of annual raises or benefits (i.e., overtime, paid vacations, sick leave, and health insurance) in this occupational sector. Because private domestic workers rarely have the option of union membership, they struggle in isolation to improve work conditions and have few opportunities to advance language or job skills. The fact that so many women are also single mothers or have partners who work outside the home means that they face the double duty of caring for children and cleaning their own homes after the paid workday is finished.

A number of studies have demonstrated that the most significant trend in domestic service over the past century has been the transition from live-in situations to day work for women.[6] Historically, live-in housework subjected domestic workers to long hours and created a problematic dependence on their employers, exposing each worker to the whims of one employer. But once they made the switch to day work, women were able to gain control over their free time as well as the structure of their workday, and ultimately they were able to change employers more freely if work conditions could not be negotiated to their liking. For the live-out domestic worker, "work and non-work life are clearly separated and the basis for employment is more clearly contractual—that is, the worker sells a given amount of labor time for an agreed-upon wage."[7]

Women enter and remain in domestic service primarily because the structure of labor markets in certain cities dictates whether other employment alternatives are available to immigrant women of education. Many of the women interviewed in Washington asserted that domestic service initially provided entree into the U.S. labor market, which, for some, meant an escape from pressing political or economic circumstances in their countries of origin. In a city such as Washington, where an unusually high proportion of women in general participate in the wage-labor force, domestic service is always available as a category of employment—even in times of recession. There are also certain advantages to domestic work that are not easily found elsewhere. Live-out domestic workers may earn higher wages and enjoy greater autonomy in determining the work pace and job conditions than do workers in other low-skill occupations (such as those in fast-food restaurants or carwashes). Several live-out domestic workers interviewed in Washington emphasized job flexibility and autonomy as the main benefits of their

Table 10   Current Employment Categories and Wages for Women

Current Job	Survey Sample (N=43)			Interview Sample (N=33)		
	N	%	Median Wages	N	%	Median Wages
Total domestic:	28	(65)*	$5.38	13	(39)*	$5.43
Housecleaning	16	(37)	5.00	5	(15)	
Officecleaning	6	(14)	5.67	7	(21)	
Baby-sitting	6	(14)	5.00	1	(3)	
Total restaurants:	4	(9)	6.75	1	(3)	5.63
Waitress	0			1	(3)	
Busgirl	1	(2)		0		
Cook	3	(7)		0		
Dishwasher	0			0		
Receptionist	0			1	(3)	5.60
Admin./secretarial	1	(2)	10.58	2	(6)	9.70
Retail/banking	2	(5)	6.38	2	(6)	4.18
Social work	0			5	(15)	7.58
Teaching	0			1	(3)	6.45

occupation, explaining that adjustable work hours and schedules allowed them to tend to children and other family responsibilities when demanded.

But domestic service has increasingly been dominated by immigrant women, who tend to become stymied in live-in housekeeping jobs and do not easily effect the transition from live-in to day work. In interviews, several women asserted that they had

(continued)

Current Job	Survey Sample (N=43)			Interview Sample (N=33)		
	N	%	Median Wages	N	%	Median Wages
Students	0			2	(6)	
Unemployed or sporadic work	2	(5)		4	(12)	
Homemaker	2	(5)		1	(3)	
Retired	0			1	(3)	
Other:	4	(9)	5.24	0		
Factory	2	(5)	4.48			
Seamstress	1	(2)	5.00			
Beautician	1	(2)	6.25			

Note: The range for women's hourly wages was $3.33 to $10.58 in the sample of 100 households, and $3.35 to $15.63 in the interview sample.
*Percentages are proportions of all women in each sample. If the numbers are calculated based on the proportion of only those women who were fully employed, the figures rise to 72 percent of women in the survey sample who currently work as domestics and 52 percent of women in the interview sample.

agreed to come to the United States to work for diplomatic families and that the families had subsequently kept the women quarantined in their homes, paid them very little and irregularly, and required them to work long hours on evenings and weekends. These women had no leverage to bargain for improved working conditions because their legal status in the United States hinged upon their ongoing employment with diplomatic families. Even in cases of extreme abuse, employers may not be prosecuted for unfair labor practices if they enjoy diplomatic immunity. Live-in domestic workers experience more acutely the many negative aspects of the profession—for example, the isolation from compatriots and other women, the dependence upon one employer, and lack of power and control over their work conditions.

Mary Romero (1992) has written extensively about the structure of paid housework and argues that many employers harbor ulterior motives for hiring women of color to clean their houses, in effect seeking to purchase status in the eyes of their neighbors and acquaintances by hiring women of color.[8] The level of servitude and submissiveness that some employers require of domestic workers impels many women—particularly U.S.-born workers—to leave the occupation as soon as other job opportunities are available. In her study of Chicana domestic workers in a West Coast city, Romero (1992:90) observed that

> Chicanas seek industry and office jobs because domestic service lacks any opportunity for advancement and because the work is monotonous and has long and irregular hours. More importantly, even though Chicanas and Mexican immigrants are usually hired for low-level and unskilled factory jobs, employers outside domestic service do not demand the same level of deference and servility. Even low paid service positions do not carry the stigma found in domestic service.

She also notes that the personal relationships between employers and employees in domestic service play a major role in determining work conditions—more so than in any other occupation—and leave workers little leverage for negotiating improvements. When employers add tasks or alter the original labor agreement in any way (such as requiring assistance with child care in addition to general housecleaning), domestic workers have little recourse for redress of grievances. Even though social networks may enable women to locate employment in domestic service whenever work is needed, such jobs tend to insulate participants from information about other occupations because of the residential and social segregation inherent in the profession.[9]

Wages for Women and Men

The work ethic for which Salvadorans in particular have earned a considerable reputation among Washington employers surfaced repeatedly in interviews with both men and women. Almost everyone reported long work histories in their countries of origin and full employment before their migration to the United States. Only 18 percent of those surveyed had worked primarily in agriculture in their countries of origin, whereas the majority emigrated from cities and arrived in the United States with skills or working trades as secretaries, teachers, business owners, production assemblers, and construction workers. An impressive proportion of the Central Americans in Washington share urban origins and are highly educated and skilled, relative to the population in their countries of origin as well as to other immigrant groups in the United States. A study of Central American immigrants residing in California noted that a significant proportion held high-status occupations and were twice as likely as adult immigrants of Mexican origin to have held white-collar jobs in their countries of origin.[10]

In the Washington area, Central American men earn markedly higher wages than Central American women even though the women have been in the United States longer (on average) and have higher education and English-language-proficiency levels than men. A majority of men also have shown measurably higher wage increases between their first jobs and their last, while most women have been segregated and locked into low-status "women's work" in domestic service. For the Central American men surveyed in Washington, sector of employment emerged as the most important influence on wage levels and employment mobility; the only personal characteristic that affected men's wages was length of time (i.e., labor market experience) in the

United States.[11] On the other hand, personal characteristics of Central American women appear (at least superficially) to have more influence on wage levels—notably education level, English-language proficiency, and legal status. But appearances of mobility are deceiving because few women were able to move out of low-status, poorly paid jobs and even fewer enjoyed sizeable increases in wages.

All of the Central American men surveyed in Washington who earned relatively high wages worked in the construction industry. The average wage for construction workers was $9.17 per hour (in 1989), the average for men who worked in restaurants was $6.25 per hour, and the average for those who worked in cleaning companies was $5.77 per hour. Construction workers earned far more than others despite the fact that a very small proportion of construction jobs in the Washington area were unionized.[12] As their social networks accurately informed them before their migration, Central American men in Washington earned markedly higher wages and experienced more mobility than Central American and Mexican men in cities such as Los Angeles and Houston. Other authors reported much lower median hourly-wage rates for immigrant men in various U.S. cities, such as $4.98 for undocumented immigrant workers in southern California in 1987–88 and only slightly more for undocumented workers who had applied for the general amnesty and possessed legal documents. Central American men in San Diego averaged $4.76 an hour in 1986; Central American men in San Francisco earned $6 on average in 1990 (primarily in restaurants and on construction sites). The highest rates of unemployment and lowest hourly-wage rates appear to accrue to undocumented Central American immigrants in Houston, where wages averaged $3.35 an hour in 1987.[13] A smaller proportion of the immigrant men studied in Houston and in Los Angeles worked in construction (11 percent and 18 percent respectively) compared with the Central American men surveyed in Washington, at 61 percent; Houston's unemployment rate was a high 12.6 percent at the time of the study in 1986 whereas

Washington's hovered around 3 percent in 1988. A majority of the Central American men in Washington found employment in large or medium-size construction companies, and a negligible number labored in fields or in sweat shops, since few agricultural and production jobs exist in the Washington area.

In order to explore the reasons why some men earned higher wages than others, I categorized Central American men into two distinct groups—those who earned high wages and those who earned low wages.[14] Within these categories, 93 percent of high-earning men worked in the construction industry, while only 36 percent of low-earnin; men worked in construction. Length of time in the United States also emerged as a factor related to high income for men; 85 percent of high earners arrived in the United States before 1986. Personal characteristics such as education level and English-language proficiency had little effect on men's wages, as Table 11 demonstrates. Both variables are comparable for low and high earners. Legal status also had little effect on men, since they were still able to secure employment in the construction and restaurant industries—generally with falsified documents—even though at least half of those surveyed were undocumented.[15] A multivariate linear regression confirmed the findings that sector of employment and length of time in the United States were the most important factors determining wage levels for Central American men. Working in construction meant that men's weekly wages rose by $88; each year of residence in the United States raised wages by $16 (see Table 12).[16]

Education levels of Central American men in Washington were significantly lower than those of Central American women; a majority of high-earning men in the survey sample had less education than most low-earning women. The Central American men who arrived in the United States with the highest levels of education—those who were attending university just before emigrating or who had attained college degrees—appear to have had less employment mobility into higher-status jobs than women with high education levels (even though men earned

Table 11 Employment Variables for Low-Earning and High-Earning Men in Both Samples

	Survey Sample		Interview Sample	
	Low-Wage* (N=28)	High-Wage* (N=27)	Low-Wage* (N=8)	High-Wage* (N=9)
Mean wage	$6.05	$10.55	$6.70	$12.23
Mean education	6.1 years	7.8	8.7	8.5
Facility w/English	86% speak none/poor	59% speak none/poor	25% speak none/poor	22% speak none/poor
Legal status	71% UD** 25% AA 4% PR	44% UD 37% AA 19% PR	13% UD 62% AA 25% PR	0 UD 100% AA 0 PR
Years in U.S.	11%>8 yrs 28% 3–8 yrs 61%<3 yrs	26%>8 yrs 59% 3–8 yrs 15%<3 yrs	62%>8 yrs — 0<3 yrs	100%>8 yrs — —
Sector of employment	36% cons*** 29% rest 14% land 14% clean 7% other	93% cons 4% retail 3% clean	25% cons 25% rest 25% land 25% other	78% cons 22% hotel (w/union)

* Hourly wages are calculated on the basis of a 40-hour work week. Low-wage workers earned less than $8.00 weekly; high-wage workers earned $8.00 or more weekly.

** UD = undocumented; AA = amnesty applicant; PR = permanent resident.

*** Cons = construction; rest = restaurant; land = landscaping; clean = cleaning.

Table 12   Regression Analysis of Factors Affecting Current Weekly
Wages for Men (sample of 100 households)

Factor	Parameter Estimate	Standard Error	P-Value
Job in construction industry	88.4	29.9	0.005
First job arranged	34.6	35.5	0.34
Found job through network	13.9	34.5	0.69
Number of years in U.S.	16.5	6.9	0.02
Number of years of education	5.8	4.1	0.16
Proficiency in English	10.5	7.8	0.56
Undocumented legal status	− 22.9	37.2	0.54

Note: Regression analysis included data solely from the survey of 100 Central
American households. Dependent variable = weekly wage. N = 57.

higher wages). Qualitative information and life histories from
the interview sample suggest that high education level may even
pose a negative factor for men's economic success. All of the
highly educated men interviewed in Washington (with 14.7 years
of schooling on average) arrived in the United States before
1982, had attained legal status, and spoke English well. Yet three
of the four men with at least a few years of college education
were among the lower earners. One man with a college degree
held a professional job as an accountant but earned only $300 a
week (or $7.50 an hour), which is half what many of the men
who worked in construction earned.

Ricardo Dominguez, the son of a Salvadoran medical doctor,
had completed three years at university while working as a professional agronomist in El Salvador. When he came to the United

States, Ricardo worked for seven years as a maintenance man at one of Washington's major universities, earning only $5 per hour. He shifted over to a job in a paint factory, where he earned $7 an hour. His classmate from El Salvador, Manuel Sosa, had finished his bachelor's degree before fleeing to the United States in 1981. Upon arrival in Washington, Manuel found a job as a laborer at a construction company and made $6.50 an hour. Dissatisfied with this type of work, he left after one year and for three years thereafter took jobs as a busboy in restaurants (at $3.50 per hour). Recently, he joined a group of Americans who had their own painting business, and at the time of the interview he was earning $9.25 an hour as a painter with legal documents. Both of these men spoke excellent English and had lived in the United States at least seven years, which made them eligible for the amnesty program and provided them with work permits. Length of time in the United States did not appear to be negative factors in their income levels. Yet none of these highly educated men had trade skills that would enable them to secure jobs in the higher-paying construction sectors, and perhaps they had little incentive to look for such jobs as readily as men with less education.

The most striking feature about Central American women's work profiles is that almost all of the women interviewed in Washington entered the labor market as domestic workers, no matter how high their education level. As shown in Chapter Three, the demand for new sources of labor for household work and child care became acute once African American women abandoned domestic service in large numbers after 1960—at a time when more and more women in general were entering the wage-labor force. Even though many Central American women had higher education levels than their male compatriots and were entrusted with the welfare of children and homes of well-to-do professionals, the women earned abysmally low wages in comparison with men (particularly as live-in domestic workers). Among those surveyed, women who worked in commercial cleaning companies earned $5.67 per hour, while the average for those who worked as domestics in private homes was $5 an hour. Hourly wages for live-out domestic workers varied between $5 and $10 an hour, comparable to the wages reported for domestic workers in California.[17] The women who worked in restaurants earned almost $7 an hour. None of the women earned over $10.60 per hour, whereas the highest earning Central American man earned $18 an hour.[18]

As with the men, I divided the women from the survey sample into two groups—high earners and low earners—in order to examine which factors might lead some women to earn higher wages than others.[19] In a statistical test, none of the personal characteristics appeared to influence women's wages to a measurable degree. The average salaries of high-earning women in both samples were almost identical, even though women in the interview sample had 1.5 more years of education, more of them spoke English, more of them possessed legal documents, and more had moved out of domestic service than those in the survey sample (see Table 13). Legal status appeared to be significant only for those women in the interview sample who had high levels of education and were able to move out of domestic service into higher-status (but not necessarily higher-paid) jobs, since all of them possessed legal documents. A regression analysis of data from the survey sample revealed that only English-speaking ability among human capital characteristics could be considered an important determinant of wages: it raised wages by $30, while education level had a negligible effect (see Table 14). Both length of time in the United States and legal status had little impact on women's wages, according to the regression analysis.[20]

The sector and industry of employment have little influence on wages for women overall because the higher-status jobs that are available to immigrant women do not pay significantly better wages for those who do effect the transition out of domestic service. A number of the women in the interview sample who held college degrees had shifted from domestic service into teaching or counseling positions at social service agencies, but these jobs paid on average $8 to $9 an hour, which is what a housekeeper

Table 13 Employment Variables for Low-Earning and High-Earning Women in Both Samples

	Survey Sample		Interview Sample	
	Low-Wage* (N=17)	High-Wage* (N=23)	Low-Wage* (N=10)	High-Wage* (N=15)
Mean wage	$4.18	$7.45	$4.00	$7.30
Mean education	8 years	9.5	8.5	11.1
Facility w/English	65% speak none/poor	52% speak none/poor	70% speak none/poor	27% speak none/poor
Legal status	59% UD** 23% AA 18% PR	43% UD 14% AA 43% PR	60% UD 30% AA 10% PR	33% UD 27% AA 40% PR
Years in U.S.	41%>8 yrs 16% 3–8 yrs 43%<3 yrs	26%>8 yrs 57% 3–8 yrs 17%<3 yrs	30%>8 yrs 20% 3–8 yrs 50%<3 yrs	53%>8 yrs 20% 3–8 yrs 27%<3 yrs
Sector of employment	82% domes* 6% rest 12% other	60% domes 9% rest 9% retail	60% domes 20% ssa 20% retail	47% domes 27% ssa 13% sec 13% other

* Hourly wages are calculated on the basis of a 40-hour work week. Low-wage workers earned less than $5.25 weekly; high-wage workers earned $5.25 or more weekly.
** UD = undocumented; AA = amnesty applicant; PR = permanent resident.
*** Domes = domestic, baby-sitting, cleaning; rest = restaurant; ssa = social service agency; sec = secretary.

Table 14   Regression Analysis of Factors Affecting Current Weekly Wages for Women (sample of 100 households)

Factor	Parameter Estimate	Standard Error	P-Value
Job as domestic (commercial)	− 8.0	25.6	0.76
First job arranged	51.6	28.6	0.08
Found job through network	30.8	22.6	0.18
Number of years in Washington	− 1.6	2.4	0.51
Number of years of education	− 3.1	3.7	0.41
Proficiency in English	30.6	14.6	0.04
Undocumented legal status	− 31.8	27.8	0.26

Note: The regression analysis did not include the four women who were unemployed or homemakers and thus was based on a sample of 39.

in a large hotel might earn after working with the same company for three or four years. In cities such as Los Angeles, immigrant women most often move into production-and-assembly jobs when they seek alternatives to domestic service. For example, Rita Simon and Margo DeLey (1986) found that over 50 percent of the Mexican immigrant women in California were working as operatives or laborers in the production sector and only 20 percent in service jobs, primarily as domestic workers. But Washington is primarily a government and "professional" city with an ample supply of service jobs, and there are virtually no production-and-assembly jobs available in the metropolitan area. Thus immigrant women find few occupations into which they might ascend that are comparable to the construction industry for men or to production jobs for immigrant women in other U.S. cities. The career path of Rosaria Lopez, detailed in the beginning of the chapter, hints at how little mobility certain categories of immigrant women may expect. Rosaria was the dressmaker from El Salvador with nine years of education who was unable to find production work in Washington and who worked two full-time jobs in order to support her family (as a domestic worker and as a seamstress in a clothing store).

Occupational Mobility

In contrast with the situation of Central American women in Washington, Central American men demonstrate laudable gains in wage levels and job status with just a few years of experience in Washington's labor market. In order to gauge mobility in wages and job status for Central American men, I measured the difference in wages between the men's first jobs and last and their movement within or between industries. Based on this difference in wages, the Central American men surveyed in Washington fell into two mobility groups—high mobility and low or no mobility. Approximately 40 percent of men demonstrated high levels of mobility, all of whom were working in the construction industry at the time of the interviews. Structural characteristics—particularly sector of employment—were clearly the most significant variables affecting occupational mobility for men (see Table 15). Length of time in the United States also influenced men's movement into higher-wage categories in the construction industry, since 67 percent of the men in the high-mobility category had arrived in the United States before 1986. But no other personal characteristics proved to be as important for men. Education level was of no consequence: 56 percent of men with wage increases had completed fewer than seven years in school, while 90 percent of men with twelve or more years of education

Table 15   Characteristics Associated with Men's Occupational
Mobility in the Survey Sample (in percent)

	High Mobility (N=18)*	Low Mobility (N=29)*
Employment in construction	100	38
Arrival in U.S. before 1986	67	55
Education longer than 6 years	44	55
Facility in English language	17	27
Possession of legal documents	39	52

* Of the 57 men in the sample of 100 households, 10 had arrived in the United
States less than one year before the time of the interview, and mobility in
wages could not be assessed.
Note: Men who averaged between $35 and $100 increase in weekly wages per
annum were classified in the high-mobility category; those who received less
than a $25 increase in weekly wages per annum were classified in the low-mo-
bility category. None of the respondents fell in between those two categories.

showed no marked increase in wages. Legal status also had little
effect on wages and occupational mobility, since over 60 percent
of the highly mobile men were undocumented. The passage of
new immigration laws (specifically IRCA) may simply impede
men's occupational mobility to the extent that, as Leo Chavez
(1992) noted, changing jobs to increase earnings may not be feasible any longer for those without legal documents.

Two of the men who were proud of their achievements and
who were among the highest earners, Jose Sandoval and Bernave
Suarez, had very little formal education. Bernave, in fact, never
attended primary school and could not read or write, nor could
he speak English well. He left El Salvador in 1981 to escape the

fighting in his home town, and after arriving in Washington he first worked in a restaurant for two years at $3.50 an hour. His brother later helped him locate a job at a construction company as a laborer (at $8 per hour) where he learned the bricklaying trade. He was subsequently able to secure a job as a bricklayer at another company at an hourly wage of $15 and aspired to be a foreman in a large construction company someday. Similarly, Jose Sandoval learned the drywall trade from coworkers on the job and, at $16 an hour, had become one of the highest-paid men among those surveyed (he had only six years of education).

Women have not experienced anything approaching the type of mobility in wages that men attain. Among the fully employed women in the survey sample, 72 percent were still working in domestic service in 1989—half of them in cleaning companies and half in private homes. To assess the factors that influence occupational mobility for Central American women, I categorized the women into two groups (high and low mobility) by measuring the difference in wages between the women's first jobs and last and movement between industries. Almost three-fourths of all Central American women experienced no mobility at all compared with only a third of Central American men who showed no mobility. Not surprisingly, 87 percent of the women in the category without mobility worked in domestic service, and length of time in the U.S. labor market made little difference for these women. Half of them had migrated to the Washington area before 1985 and still showed little or no mobility in wages or occupational status. Among the women who did experience small wage increases, 44 percent were women who had moved from private housekeeping or child-care positions into jobs with commercial cleaning companies. Only one woman in the survey sample demonstrated a high level of mobility in wages and job status on a par with the high proportion of men who did so (at 40 percent). She entered the labor market as a domestic worker and moved into a secretarial position after only three years in the United States. She had thirteen years of education, spoke English well, and arrived in the United States with legal documents because she was sponsored by a family member.

Individual life histories gleaned from the interview sample provide additional insights into the paths trod by the few women who were able to make improvements at least in job status. Women such as Rhina Garcia and Marina Suarez, two counselors at social service agencies, were considered to be highly mobile because of their movement out of domestic service into white-collar professions. Both women had earned bachelor's degrees at universities in Central America, spoke English well, and possessed legal documents. Marina worked as a domestic for only six months after her arrival in the United States and had been working as a counselor for three years while diligently attending evening classes at area universities. Marina earned $18,000 (or $8.65 an hour), while Rhina earned $14,500 (or $7 an hour)—less than Sarai Montes earned as a domestic worker in a pricey downtown hotel (at $8.50 an hour). Another former teacher at a university in El Salvador who possessed a bachelor's degree and legal documents as an amnesty applicant but who spoke little English was earning only $13,500 (or $7 an hour) as a preschool teacher. These salaries are hardly impressive compared with those of the immigrant men who worked in skilled trades in the construction industry.

All of the women in the interview sample who were considered to be highly mobile had more years of education than those with no mobility: most held college degrees or had completed between twelve and fourteen years of school, and only 14 percent still worked in domestic service. Over half of them found their current jobs through social networks, and the remaining women had college degrees and found their jobs through newspapers or employment agencies. Isabel Martinez and one other woman with a high school diploma had worked as secretaries in El Salvador. After immigrating to the United States they worked in domestic service in Washington for a number of years until both women learned enough English to make the leap into pinkcollar positions as receptionists earning $5.50 per hour. A third woman (Sarai) with a high school diploma and the same facility with English and number of years in the United States continued to work as a housekeeper in a hotel. She hoped someday to secure a secretarial position but had been unable to find one that would match the salary she earned in domestic service ($8.50 an hour). The norm appears to be that immigrant women with exceptionally high education levels and with all the human and social capital variables in their favor—such as English-language proficiency, legal status, and access to social networks—may eventually make the transition out of domestic service and into white- or pinkcollar, higher-status jobs; but because these jobs are poorly remunerated, there is less incentive to make such transitions. Social origins and class may be another hidden element in the equation, since the more highly educated Central American women tend to be from the upper classes in their countries of origin.[21]

But the women in this category form a fairly elite group; many more Central American women had moderate levels of education (six to ten years) and had once worked as semiskilled operators in their countries of origin—primarily as beauticians, seamstresses, and factory workers. For this group the job market in the nation's capital offered the bleakest outlook for mobility, since comparable employment opportunities as semiskilled workers were scarce in Washington. They simply did not find occupational sectors or employment alternatives that paid at the high levels that the construction industry did for men, nor did they have the option of factory and production work, as did immigrant women residing in cities such as Los Angeles, New York, or Miami. According to Sherri Grasmuck and Patricia Pessar (1991:175), 60 percent of Dominican women in New York work as artisans, operatives, or laborers; and 20 percent or less work in personal services (e.g., domestic service). Similar rates for operatives and domestic workers have been recorded for Mexican immigrant women in southern California.[22] Immigrant women in this semiskilled category are more likely to compete directly with other minority women—particularly with African American women—who have moved out of domestic service and into pink- or white-collar jobs. Many of these semiskilled immigrant workers are stymied in low-paying retail or service jobs in the Washington area and are forced to supplement their incomes with evening or weekend cleaning jobs. These women express a great deal of frustration over job insecurity and lack of employment mobility, and they aspire to learn new skills such as word processing so that they might eventually abandon domestic-service jobs altogether. On the other hand, women with very little formal education, such as Teresa Lopez, admit that they are content to remain in domestic service because of the flexible work hours, autonomy, and decent wages relative to what they could earn in their countries of origin.

In the past, studies of domestic service maintained that the occupation provided an important means of adaptation to urban life and to the urban labor market for women. But the view of domestic service as a "bridging occupation" facilitating horizontal and vertical mobility has proved to be illusory in both developing and highly industrialized countries.[23] Instead, recent studies on domestic workers of varying ethnic origins find that these women spend most of their working lives in the secondary or nonregulated sectors as domestic workers. Particularly in service-oriented cities such as Washington, where factory and production work is unavailable, immigrant women of color show little mobility in wage levels or occupational status. The narrow range of occupations open to them and the fact that women are often stymied in secondary-sector or nonregulated occupations only partially account for this stasis in their careers. Research on labor markets in the United States has documented patterns of gender segregation and discrimination, and Latin American women appear most vulnerable in many U.S. labor markets. One study showed that increasing proportions of immigrant women in the least-skilled job categories concurred with native-born women's mobility out of these jobs, and termed this a process of "occupational succession."[24] Another study, based on the 1980 census, found an earning gap of 29 percent between Hispanic women and white men, while the gap between Hispanic and white men was 14 percent. The conclusion drawn was that gender discrimination accounted for half the wage differential between Hispanic women and white men and that ethnicity accounted for the other half.[25]

Because of the persistent problem of gender bias in the U.S. labor market and the undervaluing of so-called women's work, the majority of immigrant women (particularly women of color) are segregated into low-paid service work and do not have access to higher-paying occupations. "Success" in the U.S. labor market depends only partially on personal motivations and abilities. How newcomers to the United States use these personal resources may depend on international political factors, the context of reception, and the types of communities created by earlier arrivals.[26] But gender factors emerge as preeminent in this analysis of immigrant labor market incorporation and render structural, cultural, and personal characteristics inadequate as explanations for the performance of Central American immigrants in the nation's capital. The labor market experiences of Central American women differ strikingly from men's, and women quickly fall far behind their male compatriots in wages and occupational mobility even though they bring many advantages with them to U.S. labor markets.

Comparisons with Other Immigrant Groups

Work patterns among Central American immigrants in the United States vary markedly from one city to another primarily because of structural differences in various labor markets, the business cycles of local economies, and gender factors operating in the labor markets. Economic conditions in the Washington area throughout much of the 1980s set the stage for the increased demand for low-wage labor, and Central American workers did not have to compete with other recent immigrant groups for most of these jobs. Similarly, a vibrant economy drew immigrants to California during the same decade, although Central Americans in that state found themselves competing with Asian, Mexican, and other Latin American immigrants for jobs. Wage levels were lower in southern California than in the Washington area for immigrant workers in comparable occupational sectors. Lower still were wage levels and labor force participation rates in Houston, since the influx of Central American immigrants to that city coincided with a severe economic downturn (particularly in the city's petro-chemical and construction industries). Nestor Rodriguez (1987) suggested that low levels of human capital, undocumented status, and poor use of social networks were constraining factors that led to low average wages among Central Americans in Houston. But for Central Americans in Washington, none of these factors militated against men's economic performance, because of the thriving local economy.

Compared to Mexican and other Latin American immigrants, Central American immigrants to the Washington area exhibit atypical labor market patterns for a number of reasons. Foremost among them is the fact that many Central Americans migrated because of political-economic conditions (often related to war) or because they or relatives were recruited to work (or had jobs arranged for them) in Washington. They are not easily categorized as manual immigrants (with low education and occupational skills) or as professional immigrants. Instead, they exhibit a wide array of personal characteristics and high averages for education and skill levels relative to Mexican immigrants.[27] In contrast to other Latin American immigrants in the United States (as well as to Central Americans in other cities), Central American men in Washington have been able to locate jobs in highly paid construction trades and to earn higher wages early on in their sojourn in this country.

Besides structural conditions in Washington's labor market, Central American men enjoy cultural advantages over other immigrant groups that may translate into relatively high wages and occupational mobility. Workers from El Salvador in particular have distinguished themselves to the extent that an element of "positive typification" surrounds them, and they enjoy a unique reputation among employers in the three sectors where they constitute a major presence in the workforce.[28] Many of the employers interviewed in Washington voiced the opinion that Salvadorans were imbued with a work ethic that made them valuable employees, and that they were diligent, hardworking, and willing to commit to longer hours on the job than employees from other ethnic or national groups. They also have earned a reputation for promptly enlisting cousins, siblings, friends, and compatriots into the workplace and making utmost use of social networks. Perhaps because of the early preponderance of women among Central American immigrants to Washington, ties to relatives and friends are brandished when job openings occur, and earlier immigrants readily assist later recruits with funds for visas and passage.[29] Another factor facilitating the incorporation of friends and relatives in Washington workplaces is that when positions become available and Central American immigrants send for relatives or friends, they are able to arrange surreptitious overland travel more easily (and at less expense) than people from more distant points.

Central American women in Washington display impressive labor force participation rates (about 80 percent) in comparison with Dominican women in New York or Mexicans in California (at 50 percent).[30] Despite pernicious labor shortages for the positions they fill and in spite of their high levels of human capital and efficient use of social networks, Central American women do not approach the wage levels of male compatriots in Washington or in certain other cities, and they are generally stymied in low-wage occupations. Gender is clearly as critical as structural or personal characteristics in determining how immigrants are incorporated into U.S. labor markets. As a result, theories about economic adjustment and labor market incorporation that are crafted on the basis of studies of immigrant men cannot simply be transposed onto the experience of immigrant women.[31]

Six

Manipulating New Immigration Laws

Once new immigrants successfully negotiate the border crossing and gain entry into the United States, the process of settling into a strange city, securing passable documents, and finding jobs ensues. Undocumented Central Americans hardly cower in fear of detention and deportation every time they venture out on the streets in the nation's capital. It is common knowledge that there are too few INS agents deployed in the Washington area to police the buses, apartment buildings, or employment sites where immigrants spend a majority of their time. Indeed, life in Washington for the undocumented appears to be far less stressful in certain aspects than for undocumented Central Americans and Mexicans in southern California. For example, Leo Chavez (1992) describes how undocumented immigrants in San Diego live with the fear that family members might be apprehended any time they venture out of their homes. The heightened state of tension exists because immigration agents are known to target buses for inspection, stop cars on the roads in order to examine documents, and even raid home sites where people live in makeshift camps. None of these practices occurs in the Washington area, and only immigrants without documents who work at high-visibility employment sites (such as restaurants or landscaping companies) fear the odd visit by INS agents. Even then, because of the ease with which work permits and social security cards may be obtained on the black market, few Central Americans in Washington are totally without documentation (see Table 16).

Lawmakers intended to make life a good deal more difficult for undocumented immigrants with the passage of the Immigration Reform and Control Act of 1986. However, they did not foresee or intend to effect a gender bias within various immigrant groups when they implemented the new law. IRCA required employers to request documents authorizing immigrants to work in the United States, and the law should have made it nearly impossible for the undocumented to find jobs any longer. But streetwise Central Americans soon developed the means of obtaining falsified documents through social networks, and relatively few were fired from or denied jobs because of a lack of employment authorization. Central American women in Washington were affected less than men by the new immigration law because a large proportion of women entered the labor market and continued to work in the nonregulated sector as household workers and child-care providers.[1] Few employers required women to show documents in order to secure such positions, and none of the women (though 11 percent of the men) surveyed in Washington were fired from a job because of IRCA. Most of the Central American immigrants in Washington agreed that it was easier for women than for men to find work after IRCA went into effect. In the long run the nationwide recession of the early 1990s was more effective at curtailing employment opportunities for newly arrived immigrants than were laboriously crafted immigration laws; but neither the recession nor IRCA had the same even impact on Central American women that they did on Central American men.

Ironically, perhaps as many employers as undocumented immigrants in the Washington area quickly devised strategies to circumvent IRCA, claiming that their ability to conduct business operations was greatly hampered by the immigration law. In

Table 16   How Documents Were Obtained by Respondents (survey sample, in persons)

	Men (N=57)	Women (N=43)
Purchased social security card in Washington, D.C.	6	3
Purchased social security card in other U.S. city	7	2
Legal social security card	5	1
Invented social security no.	2	2
Temporary work permit	11	2
Legal work permit	8	13
Employer issued false permit	0	1
Lawyers said they applied for work permit	2	1
No legal documents	6	10
No response	10	8

many cases reputable law-abiding employers resorted to the same methods that occur to international migrants who must support themselves (and families as well) by whatever means possible. Zoë Baird, President Clinton's original nominee for attorney general, was neither unique nor reprehensible when she hired two undocumented Peruvian immigrants as household helpers. Countless congressional representatives, government employees, diplomats, and other professionals in Washington and elsewhere have done the same for years and continue to hire undocumented immigrants to fill a labor vacuum for household workers. The following stories related by Washington-area employers and Central American workers illustrate the problems that both parties confront in trying to work with (or around) new immigration laws.

Claude Dejeune told of one December day in 1986 when he watched his manager greet customers at the front door of his popular Bethesda restaurant, noted for its fine French cuisine. As he strolled back to the kitchen to ensure that everything was in order before the dinner rush began, an explosion of voices erupted from the dining room. Claude backtracked through the swinging kitchen doors in time to see several men in suits chasing busboys and waiters through adjoining rooms. Dishwashers, cooks, and busboys fled toward a door leading to the back alley, but the workers ran smack into the arms of several other suited agents. Claude collided with his manager as she forged her way to the back door, following close upon the heels of a tall man in sunglasses. She was pleading with and then yelling at the man to loose his grip from the arm of one of the busboys. When the suited pursuer observed that his prey would be cornered at the back door, he turned and asked for the owner of the restaurant. Claude stepped forward and introduced himself, demanding to know what the "cowboys" were doing rampaging through his restaurant. The man snapped open his wallet, announced that he was from the Immigration Service, and stated he had information that a number of unauthorized aliens were working illegally in the restaurant. Before Claude could respond, the agent turned away and hurried toward the captives at the back door. The head chef and his assistant (both French) stood among them fumbling in their wallets for identification as several waiters attempted to explain that their identification papers were elsewhere. The rest of the kitchen staff spoke no English and averted their eyes as the INS agents interrogated them. The agents then handcuffed the busboys and dishwashers (all Salvadorans)—although they treated the French chefs with deference and declined to handcuff them—and escorted them all to waiting vans. Claude later learned that his head chef (who was undocumented) had been dating a married woman and that the tip-off to the INS came from the jealous husband. Five of the busboys and a dishwasher (all Salvadorans) were subsequently deported, as were the two French cooks.

Claude's was the first restaurant in the Washington area to be raided after IRCA went into effect. He received a warning citation after this first raid, but several weeks later the INS agents returned and once again conducted a brusque raid on his establishment. In the second raid they apprehended four undocumented workers, and Claude was fined over $3000. For several months he operated two restaurants with a severe staff shortage because of the loss of several cooks and other staff. Eventually he was forced to close one of his restaurants in order to keep the other operating at full capacity. One of his busboys, a Salvadoran who had been deported after the December raid, reappeared at Claude's restaurant two months after his deportation. He informed Claude that all of the other Salvadoran employees who were deported along with him had already returned to the Washington area and were working once again in local restaurants. When Claude related these events, he was still embittered over the new immigration law. He asserted that the only labor source available to restaurateurs such as himself were Central American immigrants because U.S.-born citizens would no longer accept dishwashing and other low-skilled jobs. He claimed he learned from this experience that "Latinos are abused in this country, more so than people of any other ethnic group. Willing workers should just be given an opportunity to work because Latin Americans don't deprive anyone of jobs in this city!"

Claude had a friend in the same business, with a pricey Georgetown restaurant (opened in 1979) who heartily affirmed these sentiments. Jean Boucher complained that he could not fill vacant positions even though he advertised constantly for a dishwasher, salad maker, and busboys. "No Americans want to do these jobs anymore," he lamented. He recounted how the previous week he ran an ad on Spanish radio advertising for dishwashers and the phone rang all day with applicants for the position. But none of the callers showed up at the restaurant when he asked them to bring work permits along to the interview. The next day he ran the same ad on the Spanish radio station, this time specifying that applicants must have work permits to apply. He received only one call in response to the ad that day. One consequence of his chronic labor shortage was that he and his managers were often left to wash the dishes or scrub floors at the end of a busy evening. Jean said that before IRCA passed, he never asked employees to show him any documents and never had vacant positions for any length of time. After IRCA, he turned away numerous job seekers who could not produce work permits. "But there are always ways," he confessed. "As long as people bring in documents that appear to be in order, I will hire them. I wouldn't know how to spot a fraudulent document and I don't care to learn," he added. "Especially when my back is against the wall, I have to improvise here to get around the law." INS agents visited Jean's establishment in 1988 simply to check on the paperwork for his employees. They noted a few errors in the I-9 forms and instructed him in detail about IRCA. "But they failed to tell me about the 'grandfather clause,' and I was worried that I would have to fire employees who were with me even before 1986. My friend Claude told me not to fire them and I did not."

Raul DeVargas founded a small drywall and carpentry business in Washington, D.C., shortly after he emigrated from Argentina in 1977. Ten years later he owned one of the largest construction companies in the metropolitan area, employing four hundred workers, of which 70 percent were from Latin American countries. Raul asserted that Central Americans already compose close to half the workforce in the area's construction industry and that by the year 2000 virtually all construction workers in the Washington area will be Latinos. "Few Americans are interested in construction work in this area," he claimed, and he described how his Anglo competitors were forced to recruit workers from Texas and Oklahoma to fill a shortage of skilled workers and of supervisors who could speak Spanish. Raul expressed his anger that "white North Americans control everything in this country and discriminate against Hispanics." Nonetheless he learned to use Anglos in visible, public positions in his company to the extent that he recruited Anglo supervisors who could speak English with his customers and Spanish with his workers. Raul maintained that all employees in his company were working legally, most of them with proper documents and some who, because they had started working with the company before 1986, were eligible to apply for permanent-resident status under the "grandfather clause." He claimed to have a personal concern for all his employees and boasted that most of his workers remained with him for years because he treated them well.

But Jose Sandoval, a Salvadoran immigrant who was interviewed in Washington, told a different story about this benevolent businessman. Jose worked for Raul's company as a drywall specialist for two years until he left the company in disgust. He asserted that many Central and South Americans worked at Raul's construction company because they had no work permits and could not find jobs anywhere else. He claimed that they were paid low wages (by Washington standards) for the work they did, but that they remained with DeVargas because of the promise that they would someday obtain legal documents through the company. Jose learned that Raul sent all his undocumented employees to one particular lawyer who, for a high fee, promised that he would file petitions for work permits. Many of the employees waited two or three years and still had no word about their applications for legal documents. Jose believed that Raul and the lawyer were in league together and that they never actually applied for papers for the undocumented workers. Jose possessed a valid work permit because he was eligible for the general amnesty program, but his younger brother had no documents when he went to work at Raul's construction company. Jose asked Raul's permission for his brother to file papers with a different lawyer, one who might process his application for a work permit quickly, but the boss denied him permission. Both Jose and his brother quit the company and Jose almost immediately found work elsewhere at higher pay. His brother took a job for less money at another company, but the management promised to process his papers rapidly. Jose blamed IRCA for enabling employers and lawyers to take advantage of undocumented workers like his brother.

These vignettes illustrate a number of the consequences that accompanied IRCA's passage, consequences that the rest of this chapter expounds upon in greater detail. Most of the employers concur that IRCA and the few high-visibility raids that followed its passage forced them to require work permits of all employees, though they suspected that the documents supplied were often fraudulent. At the very least, IRCA caused supervisors and managers to construct creative methods of juggling employees between work sites in order to circumvent the law's dictates. Employers insist that after IRCA they were forced to work with smaller staffs because there were few U.S.-born workers willing to work at low-status (ergo poorly paid) jobs any longer. On the other hand, undocumented Central American immigrants who sought formal-sector jobs claimed they must spend more time and money to acquire documents that appeared valid to their employers. The new law enhanced job insecurity, since workers could easily be fired if employers suspected they possessed fraudulent documents or if a work permit or asylum application were about to expire. The law also permitted employers like Raul DeVargas to exploit workers in a more flagrant manner than previously, since employers could pay lower wages to undocumented workers and then threaten to fire them if they complained. It enabled some employers to hold undocumented workers "hostage" with promises of legal assistance in obtaining work permits (or even permanent residency), while the employers pocketed "payments" from paychecks, ostensibly withheld for lawyers' fees. But the fallout from IRCA had a different impact on women. Any assessment of the effects of new immigration laws on immigrant workers must evaluate the gender factor as a critical element in the equation.

Changes in U.S. Immigration Law

Tens of thousands of undocumented Central American immigrants (as well as those of other nationalities) found favorable job markets in the nation's capital after 1965, a time when unprecedented changes in U.S. immigration laws went into effect. During the 1920s a national-origins quota system had established limits on immigrants from the Eastern Hemisphere, discriminating heavily against ethnic groups such as the Chinese and other Asians. But in 1965 Congress passed a law that abolished national-origin quotas and set family reunification and needed skills as the main criteria for entry into the United Sates.[2] Congress had intended that the 1965 law would maintain the existing pattern of immigration, in which 50 percent of newcomers to the United States hailed from European countries. It did not foresee that educated Asians would take advantage of the preferences for skilled workers to the extent that they did, or that both Asian and Latin American residents in the United States would encourage family members to join them in such vast numbers. After 1965 and for the first time in the nation's history, a majority of new immigrants came from third-world countries of Latin America and Asia, and by the 1980s the levels of immigration were as high as those at the beginning of the century. The total number of immigrants who arrived in the United States during the 1980s almost matched the previous record set between 1901 and 1910, when 8.8 million people entered the country. Throughout the 1980s, legal arrivals totaled about 600,000 a year, including refugees (who numbered 70,000 in 1987), while estimates on the numbers of undocumented migrants ranged between 200,000 and 500,000 annually.

Ultimately, the Immigration Reform and Control Act (IRCA) of 1986 aimed to curtail the large flow of undocumented immigrants who entered the country each year seeking employment, because many people believed that undocumented immigrants undermined standards for all workers. IRCA consisted of two main elements. The first comprised a general amnesty program that allowed the legalization of undocumented immigrants who had arrived in the United States before January 1, 1982, and had been living there continuously ever since (farm workers were allowed more lenient dates of entry under the Seasonal Agricultural Workers [SAW] program). Of the estimated four to six million undocumented aliens in the country, about half were expected to apply for the general amnesty or for the SAW program by the May 4, 1988, deadline (close to three million actually did).

The second element of IRCA entailed an employer sanctions provision that penalized employers who knowingly hired aliens unauthorized to work in the United States. This provision for the first time held employers responsible for verifying the legal status of every employee. Employers were required to verify the employment eligibility of anyone hired after November 6, 1986, to complete (within three business days of the date an employee was hired) a one-page form (the I-9) for each employee—U.S.- and foreign-born workers alike—and to retain the forms in their records. The provision applied equally to private employers and to families who employed persons for domestic work or child care in their homes on a regular basis. International migrants who arrived in the country after 1981—too late to qualify for the amnesty program—but were hired before 1986 (when IRCA went into effect) were left in a gray area covered by the so-called grandfather clause. Employers would not be fined for retaining these workers on their payroll and could apply for permanent residency for these employees, but the workers themselves could still be deported if they were apprehended by the INS.

Storefronts along 18th Street in the Adams Morgan section of Washington, where a Salvadoran restaurant shares a facade with an Ethiopian restaurant, a sports shop, and a record and tape shop. Photo by Terry Repak

Sidewalk vendors of many nationalities offer an array of goods along the streets of Adams Morgan. Photo by Anabela Garcia

Family from El Salvador waiting at a bus stop on Columbia Road in Adams Morgan. Photo by Anabela Garcia

Young mothers from El Salvador strolling the streets of Adams Morgan with their babies. Photo by Terry Repak

The Salvadoran flag floats over a stand offering *pupusas* and other Salvadoran foods at the Alexandria Hispanic Festival, June 1994. Photo by Anabela Garcia

Two young salesmen showing off electronic goods in a shop in Adams Morgan. Photo by Terry Repak

Nicaraguan women cooking and serving food from their country at the Alexandria Hispanic Festival, June 1994. Photo by Anabela Garcia

"Even Start," a program funded by the D.C. government, offers English classes to the foreign-born as well as day care for the children of students. Photo by Anabela Garcia

Central American men waiting to be picked up for day labor at the "Trailer of Silver Spring" in the Maryland suburb. Photo by Anabela Garcia

Central American men waiting for day labor at the "Trailer of Silver Spring." Photo by Anabela Garcia

A receptionist from El Salvador answers telephones at a clinic in Adams Morgan. Photo by Anabela Garcia

The Clinica del Pueblo, staffed primarily by volunteers, offers health care to members of the Spanish-speaking community. Photo by Anabela Garcia

A man from El Salvador selling music tapes from Latin America on the streets of Mount Pleasant. Photo by Anabela Garcia

A chef from Honduras preparing food at the Wharf Restaurant in Washington. Photo by Anabela Garcia

A man from Honduras cleans and buses tables at the Wharf Restaurant in Washington. Photo by Anabela Garcia

A member of a Salvadoran landscaping team working in the Washington area. Photo by Anabela Garcia

A nanny from El Salvador entertaining her young ward. Photo by Anabela Garcia

A sampling of the newspapers available to the Spanish-speaking community in the Washington area. Photo by Anabela Garcia

According to IRCA, when employers require prospective workers to submit documents that establish identity and employment eligibility,[3] the employers must decide whether documents appear to be genuine, but they are not responsible for verifying the validity of the documents. Such a wide array of documents may suffice as proof of employment eligibility (any of approximately twenty-seven pieces of information) that employers have ample excuse for accepting questionable forms of identification from prospective employees. When all else fails, employers may simply feign ignorance over the documents' validity.[4] June 1, 1988 was the date established for full enforcement of these provisions.

Numerous labor, church, and private-interest groups publicly criticized IRCA, arguing that the cut-off date for the general amnesty should have been set closer to the date when the new law passed (about 1986), because the law discriminated heavily against recent arrivals such as immigrants from El Salvador and Guatemala. They contended that the arbitrary date mandated for the amnesty deadline allowed only half the undocumented immigrants in the United States to apply for legalization, leaving millions of people who would still be subject to deportation and who would be more vulnerable to exploitation by employers than in the past.[5] Employers objected that the added paperwork and expenses incurred in complying with the law were burdensome and forced them to hire additional personnel just to fill out I-9 forms and to watch for expiration dates on temporary work permits.

Apart from the amnesty program under IRCA and the preference categories for relatives of U.S. citizens, there are several alternative routes by which undocumented immigrants may obtain authorization to work in the United States. One of the most common means of obtaining permanent-residence status (signified by the possession of a "green card") is for an employer to agree to "sponsor" someone by filing a petition on his or her behalf.[6] A majority of the Central American women interviewed in Washington who became permanent residents before the amnesty program took effect had been "sponsored" by families for whom they were working as housekeepers or child-care providers; fewer Central American men were able to find sympathetic employers who were willing to "sponsor" them for labor certification. New arrivals may also obtain temporary work authorization once they apply for political asylum.[7] Many Salvadorans, Guatemalans, and Nicaraguans were forced to use this method throughout the 1980s, especially if they faced deportation proceedings. During the worst years of the protracted and brutal civil war in El Salvador, as few as 2.7 percent of the Salvadorans who applied were granted political asylum in the United States (between 1984 and 1988), because the Justice Department under President Reagan was authorized to deport most of the Salvadorans detained by the INS.[8] But a bill that took effect in 1990 granted eighteen months of Temporary Protective Status (TPS) to all undocumented Salvadorans and Guatemalans in the United States (the deadline was later extended).[9]

The underlying intent of the Immigration Act of 1990 (ImmAct) was to reform permanent legal immigration at a time when the United States admitted approximately a half million immigrants annually. ImmAct increased that amount to a permanent annual level of 675,000 immigrants, with family reunification still the defining feature of United States immigration policy. Family and refugee immigrations account for about five-sixths of total legal immigration to the United States. ImmAct made additional changes in employment-based immigration by facilitating the speedy entry of professional and highly skilled immigrants and increasing the number of permanent employment-based labor certifications from 54,000 to 140,000. It also made permanent provision for the admission of "diversity immigrants" from underrepresented countries. Whether this new law will have the unintended gender bias that surfaced after the passage of IRCA remains to be seen.

IRCA's Impact on Employers

Stefan Viola, owner of a fashionable Italian restaurant in Washington, D.C., espoused the well-worn cliché that "the United States is a country of immigrants and a land of opportunity." He believed that any human being who was willing to work hard should have the chance to realize the American dream as he had, since "America is still a rich country capable of helping others." He vigorously proclaimed:

> I myself came to this country as an illegal immigrant. If that law [IRCA] was passed a hundred years ago, the men who passed it would still be in Europe today. Even congressmen are descendants of immigrants. We need the poor immigrants here more than the rich professionals. A guy from El Salvador doesn't know if tomorrow he can survive so we need to let the poor people from El Salvador work here, just like we let the immigrants have a chance a hundred years ago.

To what extent these sentiments issue from his own self-interest—that is, his ability to employ more workers at low wages—or from a heartfelt identification with immigrant workers is an insoluble conundrum. Stefan Viola's restaurant was raided by INS agents in 1975, and seventeen of his employees working in the country illegally were detained in that raid. Stefan posted bond for all of them and subsequently sponsored sixteen of the workers for labor certification, which helped them attain permanent residency (one person decided to return home voluntarily). He believed in helping his employees because "I can see the human side and I think they [lawmakers] are blocking the opportunities for good people who want to work. These are the people who made America great and they help to revitalize this country!"

Another Washington restaurateur who was born and raised in Tennessee called himself a staunch Republican but said that he had learned from experience how messy the U.S. immigration system is.

> I feel badly for the Salvadorans and other people who come from conflict areas and I'll do anything to help them. I think our country is responsible for many of the problems in their countries. They'll never be able to stop illegal immigration completely, and they should stop spending so much money on trying to catch people who are already here. They have to come up with a better system.

On behalf of his employees this restaurant manager spent hours at INS offices, dealing with paperwork and tracking documents that were lost by the INS, as well as dispensing large amounts of money on legal fees trying to help his employees obtain documents that permit them to work in the United States.

Few of the employers in the construction, restaurant, or cleaning industries who were interviewed in Washington expressed any ambivalence about IRCA.[10] Like Claude Dejeune, Jean Boucher, and Stefan Viola, many employers felt justified in skirting the law in order to satisfy their business needs or because they disagreed with its stated intent and method of enforcement. Among the twenty-five construction-company employers interviewed, for example, few admitted that they continued to employ undocumented workers, and all employers claimed that they required potential employees to show documentation in order to fill out the I-9 forms. Yet 61 percent of the Central American men surveyed in Washington worked in the construction industry, and at least half of them were undocumented. Many of the undocumented immigrants asserted that their employers never asked to see any documentation. On the other hand, almost half of the employers in the thirty-five restaurants visited admitted that they retained undocumented workers on the payroll, many of the employers explaining that they had no choice but to keep undocumented workers because of the severe labor shortage in the region. Both construction and restaurant industry employers confessed they were aware that fraudulent documents were common among Central American immigrants in the Washington area, and these employers conceded that they did not attempt to verify whether documents were legal or fraudulent (see Tables 17 and 18).

At one large cleaning company in Washington that employed over two thousand workers, 80 percent of the employees were from Latin American countries, and the turnover in the workforce was extremely high—approximately six hundred workers per month. Such an enormous turnover rate might well be indicative of poor working conditions or unacceptably low wages. Yet the company's manager, Arletta Smith, claimed that her company had yet to experience a labor shortage, because somehow her supervisors always produced enough workers when they were needed. "People who want to work will simply find ways," she quipped. Arletta speculated about some of the methods the supervisors devised in order to secure enough workers to clean buildings under contract with her company. For special short-term contracts, workers could be hired without requiring work permits if they were employed for only one, two, or three days. Or a documented worker who planned to leave the company might send a relative or a friend in to work under the original employee's name (thereby "selling" the positions). Some supervisors even juggled undocumented workers between different buildings, letting them work for three days in one, three in another, and so on. Arletta was unconcerned whether her employees were undocumented or in possession of fraudulent documents. She argued that the turnover rate of six hundred employees a month indicated that "they simply don't stay long enough [for her] to worry about documents." She also believed that INS enforcement in the cleaning industry would be extremely difficult, since most people work at night in buildings that have countless numbers of closets, offices, and potential hiding places (see Table 19).[11] Arletta maintained that "all this law has done is to create an illegal black market in paperwork. We had a problem for the first six months [after IRCA went into effect], but then all of these people started coming in with perfect documents. I don't know where they're getting them, but I would

Table 17   Construction Company Responses to IRCA Questions (by ethnicity of ownership)

	Hispanic-Owned (N=10)		Non-Hispanic-Owned (N=15)	
	N	%	N	%
Required documents	(10)	100	(15)	100
Admitted having undocumented workers	(1)	10	(0)	
Sponsored employees	(8)	80	(5)	33
Mean number of employees sponsored	(7.5)		(4.8)	
Fired employees because of IRCA	(6)	60	(4)	27
Mean number of employees fired	(3.5)		(10)	
Experienced difficulty finding employees	(5)	50	(12)	80

stand up in court and testify that they're as legal as I can determine."

One cleaning-company owner of Latin American origin claimed that he lost over half of his workforce because of IRCA. He was afraid to risk hiring undocumented workers after hearing about INS raids on other companies in the area, because his business would be bankrupt if he had to pay an exorbitant fine. Another Spanish-speaking employer in a cleaning company

(continued)

	Hispanic-Owned (N=10)		Non-Hispanic-Owned (N=15)	
	N	%	N	%
Blamed IRCA for labor shortage	(5)	50	(8)	53
Labor shortage hurt business	(3)	30	(10)	67
Believe Latinos will dominate in industry	(10)	100	(9)	60
Believe Latinos already dominate in industry	(6)	60	(1)	7
Visited by INS	(5)	50	(3)	20
Fined by INS	(3)	30	(0)	
Warned by INS	(0)		(1)	7
Want IRCA changed	(9)	90	(12)	80

claimed that Latin Americans constituted 80 percent of his workforce and that he had to fire many of his Salvadoran workers after IRCA passed, because they lacked the proper documentation. He was hurt both by competition in the area and by IRCA and could not expand his business or take on any new contracts, because of his difficulty in finding documented workers. An employer in a large nonunion cleaning company said that the

Table 18   Restaurant Employers' Responses to IRCA Questions (by ethnicity of ownership)

	Hispanic-Owned (N=15)		Non-Hispanic-Owned (N=20)	
	N	%	N	%
Required documents	(14)	93	(18)	90
Admitted having undocumented workers	(6)	40	(6)	30
Sponsored employees	(12)	80	(15)	75
Mean number of employees sponsored	(3)		(10)	
Fired employees because of IRCA	(5)	33	(8)	40
Mean number of employees fired	(3.6)		(3)	
Experienced difficulty finding employees	(9)	60	(16)	80

company's turnover rate was very high—as much as 50 percent per year. This employer experienced grave problems with labor shortages and as a result was unconcerned whether workers possessed fraudulent documents. In contrast, the one cleaning company I visited where most of the employees belonged to a union reported a low turnover rate and no semblance of a labor shortage.

Unlike cleaning companies, restaurants are high visibility job

(continued)

	Hispanic-Owned (N=15)		Non-Hispanic-Owned (N=20)	
	N	%	N	%
Blamed IRCA for labor shortage	(9)	60	(12)	60
Labor shortage hurt business	(8)	53	(13)	65
Visited by INS	(8) (1 pre-IRCA) (2 for info/I-9 check)	47	(10) (4 pre-IRCA)	50
Fined by INS	(0)		(2)	10
Warned by INS	(2)	13	(2)	10
Workers seized	(2)	13	(5) (3 pre-IRCA)	25
Wants IRCA changed	(15)	100	(15)	75
No response	(0)		(2)	10

sites for foreign workers and pose easier targets for INS raids. Over half of the thirty-five restaurant employers interviewed in Washington claimed that they were subjected to unannounced INS visits, a majority after IRCA passed in 1986. Eight employers recalled raids in which their workers were physically detained by INS agents. Claude Dejeune's restaurant was only the first in a number of high-profile raids on area restaurants. An executive

Table 19 Cleaning-Company Responses to IRCA Questions

	Company Number				
	1	2	3	4	5
Annual sales volume ($)	300,000	not avail	not avail	9,000,000	20,000,000
Type of cleaning	govt.	comm.	comm.	comm.	comm.
Age of company (yrs.)	7	15	30	17	30
No. full-time employees	10	200	300	300	450
No. part-time employees	58	100	1,700	100	2,550
Union contractors	no	many	no	few	no
Women employees	85%	60%	50%	50%	75%
Latino employees	80%	20%	80%	20%	24%
Starting wage	$4.75 night 6.00 day	$5.00	$4.75 DC 4.50 Md/ Va	$4.75 DC 5.00 Md/ Va	$4.75 DC 5.00 Md/ Va

Increase over 3 yrs.	1.00	0.25	1.00	1.00	1.40
Required documents	no	yes	yes	yes	yes
Undoc. employees now	no	no	probably	unsure	no
Sponsored employees	yes	no	yes	no	yes
Fired employees because of IRCA	yes	no	yes	no	yes
Labor shortage?	yes	no	some	yes	yes
Blamed IRCA for labor shortage	yes	no	initially	yes	yes
Labor shortage hurt business	yes	no	no	yes	yes
Latinos replacing American workers	yes	no	yes	N.R.	no
Visited by INS	no	no	yes (info)	yes (info)	no
Fined by INS	no	no	no	no	no
Wants IRCA changed	yes	yes	yes	yes	yes

Note: govt. = government; comm. = commercial; N.R. = no response.

of a company that owns a national chain of restaurants related how INS agents raided several of his restaurants in 1988, detaining thirteen undocumented workers from one restaurant and nine from another. The agents inspected 2,200 files on employees and imposed a $60,000 fine on the company for improperly maintained I-9 forms and for employing undocumented workers. The Justice Department brought criminal charges on twenty-four counts against the company for harboring "illegal aliens," charges that were eventually dropped when contested in court. The company's president contended that the raids on his restaurants were a scam intended to frighten other restaurant owners. "We were big enough to be visible but small enough for the INS to tackle," he asserted. At six other restaurants, INS agents simply dropped in to check on the employers' I-9 forms to determine whether they were correctly filled out for each employee, and several other restaurants received visits offering instruction on the fine points of IRCA. These restaurateurs all maintained that the INS agents failed to apprise them of the grandfather clause, which would allow them to retain employees who had been working for them since before 1986.

INS levied a hefty fine on only one employer among the construction companies I visited in the Washington area, and smaller fines on two other companies. The owner of the first company (a man of Latin American origin) was forced to pay $15,000 for four undocumented workers, and he contended that contractors with Hispanic surnames were scrutinized more thoroughly than his Anglo competitors. In fact, all three of the contractors I visited who said that they were fined for IRCA-related violations were men of Latin American origin.

Why would many respectable business owners willingly break the immigration laws of the United States in order to continue hiring undocumented workers? Ostensibly, the motivation compelling such conduct was a labor shortage in the Washington area that persisted throughout most of the 1980s. The shortage of particularly skilled labor in the construction industry was so severe, for example, that employers had to devise new recruitment strategies to meet their manpower needs. Nearly half of the construction company employers interviewed said they recruited workers in Texas, Oklahoma, and other states during the 1980s, or they simply hired workers from those states who journeyed to Washington in search of jobs between 1986 and 1988. One employer who moved to Washington from Dallas in 1986 explained that "skilled workers are harder to find here than in Dallas." He imported a dozen skilled workers when he moved from that city, most of whom returned to Texas within two or three years. Another employer agreed that "workers coming from Texas take jobs at very low wages—30 to 40 percent lower than D.C. workers—and this helps the competition a lot."

As many as three-fourths of the construction industry employers interviewed in Washington believed that workers from Latin American countries predominated in most of the construction trades in the nation's capital because of the labor shortage. But nearly as many asserted that workers of Latin American origin did not deprive U.S.-born workers of jobs.[12] They simply saw no alternative willing and qualified labor sources available around the Washington area apart from Central and South American immigrants. Most of the employers explained that they primarily used networks to recruit new workers, and their employees tended to send friends and relatives of the same nationality or ethnic group when new positions became available. Only three of the twenty-five construction companies I visited were closed shops and hired primarily through unions; they were among the largest companies in the area (two of the three were owned by men of Latin American origin) and none of them complained about a labor shortage.[13]

Like their counterparts in the construction industry, three-fourths of the restaurant owners interviewed in Washington claimed they experienced difficulty in recruiting enough employees to staff their restaurants. Many attributed their difficulties to IRCA and insisted that the law severely hurt the restaurant industry in the Washington area. When asked whether they attempted to recruit alternative sources of labor, restaurateurs of Latin American origin gave responses sharply different from those of their U.S.-born counterparts. One employer believed that "no African American is going to be happy having a Latin boss." She asserted that Americans were unwilling to work at the pace required in her restaurant, juggling several different jobs on any given night. "A waiter has to be able to bus tables and even to help with dishwashing when we are short a few workers, and few North Americans are willing to do multiple jobs," she explained. She claimed that she preferred to risk hiring undocumented workers if documented Latin American employees were unavailable when she needed them. Three other employers of Latin American origin echoed her sentiments and explained that because their businesses catered to the Spanish-speaking community, workers of Hispanic-origin were the only suitable labor source—even if they were undocumented workers. Two restaurateurs who had experienced a long labor shortage admitted to actively recruiting (or "stealing") workers from other restaurants. All of the employers agreed that immigrants of Latin American origin responded to newspaper ads for kitchen help more frequently than any other group of workers. A man who owned two Middle Eastern restaurants complained that as a result of IRCA he was considering closing one of his restaurants rather than continually worrying about how to fill staff positions. Several employers admitted that they intended to welcome undocumented employees in their restaurants in the future and to sponsor as many as they could in order to help good workers prosper.

A labor shortage is also what forces many private employers and working parents like Zoë Baird to disregard whether prospective housekeepers or child-care workers have legal work permits. All five of the employers interviewed in companies that secured nannies and housekeepers for private families said that families residing in the Washington area had an acute need for

domestic workers and child-care providers given the large proportion of women in the workforce. Every one of these employers said that he or she maintains a long list of families waiting
for nannies or housekeepers and that many of the families are
willing to sponsor foreign-born workers for labor certification.
One employer contended that while most of the Latin American
women who answered her ads were able to produce some documentation, she could place many more people if it were not for
IRCA. Only one of these five employers maintained that she re-
ferred only women with green cards as nannies even though she
had a waiting list with three hundred families on it. She claimed
that many Washington-area women who wanted to work were
forced to stay at home because of the lack of adequate child care.
She lamented that "this law is making common criminals of
American families and good hardworking people who just want
to work! I think the law was poorly written and should be
amended. The general-amnesty provision let in an underclass of
people when the law should have granted work permits to people on a conditional basis."

IRCA's Impact on Immigrant Workers

Like their employers, Central American workers without legal
documents were caught in a contradiction when Washington's
booming local economy beckoned with assurances of high-
paying jobs but the dictates of the new immigration law sought
to prevent them from working at such jobs. How deeply the law
affected undocumented immigrants and families in general is a
much debated issue, yet little has been written about the uneven
impact it may have on immigrant women as opposed to immigrant men. Initially, by shifting the burden of proof onto immigrants (to show that they were qualified to hold a job in the
United States), the law appeared to enhance the difficulties for
all undocumented immigrants who were seeking employment.

Restaurant owner Jean Boucher, for example, related how dozens of applicants for positions in his restaurant failed to appear for interviews when he asked them to bring work permits along with them. He admitted that a few months after IRCA took effect, prospective employees came to him with work permits that might well have been fraudulent.

But IRCA did not have the same impact on immigrant women as it did on immigrant men in the Washington area. While 40 percent of the employers interviewed in the construction, restaurant, and cleaning industries claimed that they were forced to fire undocumented workers because of IRCA, only 11 percent of the Central Americans interviewed admitted that they were fired from a job because of IRCA (see Table 20). Most of these respondents were men who worked in the construction industry. Because a majority of immigrant women were employed in private households as domestic workers, few employers required them to show documents in order to obtain jobs or fired them after IRCA passed. In fact, the INS even issued a statement after the Zoë Baird flap to assure families who employed domestic workers that no private households in the Washington area had ever been fined for IRCA-related violations. In effect, Central American women who work in domestic service are shielded from the immediate effects of IRCA even though the work environment of private households isolates them and offers few opportunities for employment mobility from informal- to formal-sector jobs.

Most of the Central American men and women interviewed in Washington claimed they did not know any compatriots who left the United States voluntarily because of IRCA; instead, they maintained that people simply moved in with other relatives if they had temporary difficulties with employment. Only two women reported that they knew of people who returned to El Salvador or Guatemala because they did not qualify for the general amnesty under IRCA or because they could not find jobs after the passage of IRCA. Two of Isabel Martinez's brothers were deported after INS agents apprehended them at their job sites (in

Table 20   Impact of IRCA on Respondents in the Survey Sample
(in percent)

	Yes	No	No Response
Aware of IRCA?	76	24	0
Fired because of IRCA?	11	85	4
Employers ask to see documents before hiring	55	45	0
Problems with documents?	20	79	1
Problems because of IRCA?	20	79	1
INS visited job site?	9	90	1
INS fined employer?	1	95	4
Friends/relatives returned home because of IRCA?	25	74	1
Friends/relatives deported because of IRCA?	21	77	2
Basic needs increased because of IRCA?	5	94	1

construction) and found that they did not have legal work permits. Marina Suarez, the counselor at a social service agency, joked about the number of young men she knew who were deported but simply returned as soon as they could afford the trip back to Washington. One person she knew claimed to have been deported five times and bragged that nothing could stop him from returning to the United States.

At the very least, IRCA certainly shifted the burden of adjustment from its intended target (employers) to individual immigrants and families, and families and community agencies were forced to pick up the slack in supporting and helping new arrivals. For example, countless parishioners in Washington's churches sheltered immigrants from El Salvador during the war years until they could find housing and jobs on their own. Several undocumented Central Americans complained in interviews that they had to rely more heavily on social service agencies and churches for food, housing, and job information and that work conditions became less stable and job mobility more tenuous—particularly for men who worked on high-visibility job sites accessible to INS inspection (e.g., at construction sites or in restaurants). The process of obtaining a social security card and fraudulent work permits also became more expensive and cumbersome than it used to be for both women and men. Monico Lopez and Jose Sandoval recalled that back in 1980 they purchased social security cards for $10 soon after they arrived in the Washington area. Now new arrivals may have to pay $20 to $35 for a social security card, and from $200 to $600 for a falsified work permit.[14] A Labor Department investigation confirmed that "the need to find and purchase documents . . . led to a greater reliance on network recruitment and to a longer wait to locate a first job. There was a resultant increased demand on families and communities to support new arrivals in this extended period of document and job search."[15]

But IRCA has failed to achieve the bulk of its stated intentions. It has not led to substantial increases in wages for undocumented workers who qualified for the general amnesty, according to the Central Americans interviewed in Washington.[16] In the long run, IRCA's impact on current migration patterns has been minimal at best because, according to several official reports, potential immigrants simply waited to see how the law worked and then began moving again. Wayne Cornelius noted, "There has been no significant return flow of illegals who suddenly found themselves jobless in the U.S. [In the short term at least, the 1986 law] may have kept more Mexicans in the U.S. than it has kept out."[17] Another report concluded that at all of the research sites for a lengthy study on the impact of employer sanctions, "the influx of new unauthorized workers continued with virtually no indication of a change and, as especially anticipated by the Law, a decline in the volume of arrivals."[18] Social service agency representatives asserted that the law enhanced conditions of instability in the labor market by making it possible for employers to rid themselves of unwanted workers if the workers were undocumented. IRCA failed to stem abuses by employers like Raul De-Vargas, who purportedly paid his undocumented workers less than those with work permits and who made vague promises to help them obtain legal documents, while extorting monthly sums from them for "legal fees."

Marina Suarez related accounts of several undocumented immigrants who for years suffered other forms of abuse by employers before they sought help at her social service agency. She told of how Pablo Gonzalez ventured into her office one day along with his cousin (both of them from Guatemala) after he summoned the courage to visit a social service agency. Pablo and his cousin were only sixteen years old when a neighbor in their tiny Guatemalan town informed them of a man who worked through the Sanctuary Movement to help young people escape difficult conditions in their countries of origin. Pablo begged the man to help him make the journey to the United States but informed him that he had no money or contacts in that country. The man arranged to send Pablo, his cousin, and several other boys to Washington, D.C., where they would be met by a Guatemalan man who would employ them and give them shelter. Juan Vasquez was a subcontractor in the Washington area in constant need of painters for his company. Pablo claimed that he lived with five other boys as virtual prisoners in Juan's house for almost two years. They slept on the floor of the family's basement, received only one meal a day, and were forced to work twelve to fourteen hours every day without food on the job sites. Juan often warned the boys that something bad would happen to their families in Guatemala if they told anyone about their conditions or if they demanded money for their work. They were never paid any wages at all. Pablo spoke of how depressed they were for months and how all the boys were afraid to write home because of Juan's threats and because of their shame in having no money to send to their families. One day Juan sent them to work for a general contractor who paid them a pittance for painting a house, and at that job site they finally grasped the opportunity to escape. A friend convinced them that it was safe to tell their story to someone at an agency assisting young people from Latin American countries. Marina then persuaded the boys to render their testimony to officials in order that Juan might be prosecuted for abusive treatment of juvenile workers. She negotiated with INS and FBI agents, who agreed to grant them immunity from deportation for their cooperation, but neither agency ever followed through on the investigation and the FBI failed to prosecute Juan on any charges. Meanwhile Marina helped the boys to locate paid employment and housing elsewhere in Washington.

Another of Marina's clients left three children in El Salvador in order to work in the United States for a few years. The woman (Adela Sandria) first made her way to Texas, where she secured a job with a family that moved frequently about the United States. The family took Adela to live with them when they moved to a farm in Pennsylvania, and they kept her there (against her will) under lock and key for four years. They expected her to care for the family's four children and allocated her a corner in the bedroom of the two youngest children so that she could attend to them if they awoke in the night. She received no payment in the four years that she worked for them, despite the fact that she was responsible for all the cooking, cleaning, and child care for the family. They did not allow her to use the telephone or to venture out of the house even to attend church, and because no one around her spoke Spanish, she was unable to complain to outsiders about her plight. She missed her children and was depressed that she was not able to send any money for their support. After four years of this treatment Adela accompanied the family on a visit to Texas over the Christmas holidays. One afternoon when her employers were distracted with Christmas shopping in a crowded mall, Adela saw her chance to escape and slipped away from the family. She was able to phone a cousin in Houston, who immediately retrieved her and then housed her for several weeks. The cousin offered Adela the money to travel to Washington, D.C., where another cousin could help her find a job. At the time of this narrative, Adela (who was without legal documents) worked at a fast food restaurant in Washington and complained that she was still mistreated by her employers. The supervisor forced Adela and other undocumented workers to report for work at a certain hour, and then ordered them to wait until the restaurant was very busy before they were allowed to punch the time clock. She claimed that she often worked twelve hours a day but was paid for only six.

Marina also related accounts of foreign-born women who were brought to Washington to work for diplomatic families and subsequently treated as indentured servants. Many of these women were afraid to complain because their legal status hinged upon their employment with the families; the employing families enjoyed diplomatic immunity and could not be prosecuted for mistreating household workers. These types of abuses existed long before IRCA became law and will probably continue as long as there is a vulnerable workforce of undocumented workers willing to accept low wages.

Resistance versus Noncompliance

When legions of workers from other countries remain undocumented in the United States, unaffected by legislation such as IRCA and unprotected by U.S. laws, they remain liable to abuse from employers. While the new immigration law ostensibly set

out to protect North American jobs for qualified workers,
IRCA's designers omitted protections for large numbers of individuals who were already an integral part of the labor force in
various U.S. cities. Nonetheless IRCA did not pose an impassi-
ble barrier to employment for most undocumented immigrants
in the Washington area before the recession altered the regional
labor market canvas after 1989, as the extremely low unemployment rate among them demonstrates. In follow-up interviews five years after the initial interviews were conducted, three
women blamed the recession for the plight of partners who lost
jobs in the construction industry, illustrating the uneven effects
of recession on immigrant women and immigrant men. Even in
difficult times, private employers of domestic workers and child-
care providers apparently consider such services indispensable,
so that immigrant women may be insulated from the ripple effects of recession to a greater degree than men.

Is it valid when Washington-area employers complain that
they wrestle with a labor shortage in a city where African Americans constitute an overwhelming majority of its residents and
unemployment rates for this group hover around 7 or 8 percent?
Employers in restaurants and in cleaning and child-care services
universally voiced the opinion that "Americans don't want to do
this type of work any longer." What some employers of Latin
American origin admitted confidentially is that they did not believe African Americans were good workers or got along well
with employees of Latin American origin. For a number of years
the Washington area certainly experienced a tight labor market
in which job growth outweighed any accompanying expansion
in population. Yet equally salient is the fact that certain occupational categories (especially in the restaurant, cleaning, and
child-care industries) are notoriously underpaid besides being
low-status, labor-intensive professions. Few U.S.-born workers,
including African Americans, are willing to accept such demanding work at low pay and with little opportunity for advancement. In time IRCA may force wages to increase margin-

ally for dishwashers, busboys, domestic workers, and child-care providers but probably not to an extent that would entice U.S.-born workers back to these occupational sectors.

Predictably, a majority of employers voiced the hope that IRCA might eventually be changed or abolished.[19] They fundamentally opposed the notion that employers should be responsible for controlling immigration—a task that they believed could be performed more efficiently at the border. As one employer lamented, "It's not so much the law that's the problem but the way it's implemented. It forces us to do the police work for the government, and why should I have to do their surveillance work? Soon they'll be fining me if my employees use drugs!" More caustic complaints about the negative impact of IRCA tended to come from small business owners and restaurateurs. Small general contractors in construction and commercial cleaning companies, for example, asserted that they were no longer able to bid on future contracts because they could not be sure that they would find enough workers to complete proposed projects. They were forced to finish one job before bidding on others and to take a piecemeal approach to their work that shortened horizons in planning for the future. Only larger construction companies were still able to secure contracts well in advance of a project and to forecast their labor needs a year or more ahead of time. A report issued by the Department of Labor confirmed these findings for other cities and locations throughout the United States. "Firms that are larger, more stable, and pay higher wages have no problems with IRCA or with labor shortages that in the future could be linked to employer sanctions. Small, ethnically-owned, competitive firms and markets experience greater difficulties."[20]

Overall, studies of labor markets in New York, Los Angeles, Washington, Houston, and rural areas throughout the Southeast and the Midwest show that the employer sanctions provision of IRCA had few of the intended effects for reshaping the workplace to deter unauthorized immigration. A Labor Department report summarized:

The Law failed to make legal status an enforceable employment standard for which employers were held accountable. Pervasive, systematic use of unverifiable, fraudulent documents made it unnecessary for employers to comply with little more than the paperwork provisions of the Law. New arrivals continued to present themselves for employment in the labor markets we studied, and those who could not obtain appropriate documents were still able to locate some form of work.[21]

Over time, employers and undocumented immigrants alike have concocted various methods of resistance to a law that they consider to be unjust at worst and meaningless at best.

Seven

New Roles in a
New Landscape

The entire process of migration incites dramatic transformations in women's and men's attitudes about their work, their gender roles, and relationships within the family. Wage work in the United States is simply one change-inducing element in a broader social-cultural context where women find themselves transformed through the processes of migration and settlement. In tandem, migration and labor force participation in the United States effectively erode the political and economic basis of patriarchal authority, since men rarely perform as sole heads of households upon settlement in this country. The balance of power between men and women in family structures shifts as women gain greater personal autonomy, independence, and decision-making leverage from their participation in the labor force and in community life. Men, on the other hand, are forced to share authority, decision-making, and sometimes even household responsibilities (albeit unevenly) with women, particularly if women are employed full-time outside the home.[1]

For many Central American women, wage work was already an accepted norm (as well as a matter of economic survival), and they faced fewer cultural sanctions against women in the wage-labor force in their home countries than other women of Latin American origin confronted at home.[2] Political and economic conditions in certain Central American countries that set the stage for migration to the United States had already eroded some of the patriarchal and societal strictures that would have inhibited women from active participation in the wage-labor force or in community activities. As few immigrant households were able to survive in the Washington area without the financial contribution of women's wages, these women became direct actors in the labor market and in their communities immediately upon resettlement.

This chapter documents the ways in which the migration and work experiences that women encounter in the United States foment profound transformations in perceptions about their identities as wage earners, about gender roles in relationships, and about career aspirations.[3] As Consuela Mendez, a divorced mother of two children from El Salvador observed,

> Men need women more here, economically speaking, because they can't get by very easily without women working. They need women's wages and they have to help more in the house, even taking care of the children more because there is not much money for child care. Also, men can't go after other women as easily here because they can't support two families at one time and they have to work too hard. So I think it's better for women here.[4]

Yet many Central American women trade one set of contradictions (such as performing as wage earners and/or single heads of households in traditional Catholic cultures) for an altogether different set of contradictions upon resettlement in the United States. Reverberations from the migration process in the work-family nexus are manifest in the different responses of immigrant women and immigrant men to the myriad changes that the migration and settlement processes engender.

Transforming Gender Roles and Relationships

Studies conducted in a variety of racial-ethnic communities have demonstrated that women's paid employment and economic contribution to the family enhance self-esteem and decision-making leverage for immigrant women at the same time as it burdens them with the assumption of double and triple roles.[5] In particular, the literature on women and migration has already described some of the ways in which the migration process enables women to renegotiate their relationships and gender roles with men—in decisions concerning labor force participation, in control over the household budget, and in the division of labor within the household. Once women become aware of the advantages that the migration process may confer on them, this role renegotiation may even provide inducement for migration. A study of Dominican immigrants, for example, found that many women veiled their reasons for migration under such explanations as "I wanted to join my husband" or "We wanted our family to be together in one place."[6] Family reunification was generally a subterfuge for more personal goals as many Dominican women sought to alter circumstances in their country of origin that left them totally dependent on men's earnings within the household. These women sought to attain greater decision-making power and control over their lives through migration and labor force participation in the United States, where fewer sanctions against women in the work force exist. Fernández-Kelly and Garcia (1988:2) observed that many Mexican women entered the labor force in the United States because they could not survive on men's earnings alone or because they had been abandoned by male partners. As a result, when the Mexican women were thrust into positions of financial autonomy, "disillusion about the viability of men as economic actors [could] translate into greater receptivity to ideals and hopes of personal emancipation, progress and financial independence."[7]

Like the Mexican women in the California study, Central American women in Washington often entered the wage-labor force as single heads of households or as essential contributors to the family's economic survival. For those who were married, the traditional ideology that cast men in the role of sole bread-winner had to be jettisoned at the onset of the settlement process in the United States because families were simply unable to survive on one income. The labor force participation rate of Central American women in Washington is extremely high (at 87 percent) because of economic necessity and because many women prefer to earn their own income in order to acquire material goods and to maintain personal autonomy. As typologies of traditional male/female wage-earner roles erode, control over the household budget and the division of duties within households become pivotal points of dispute for many immigrant families. The Dominican women in New York who pooled incomes with their partners, for example, were able to enhance their control over domestic resources and shift toward a relatively egalitarian division of labor inside the home.[8]

All but one of the Central American women who were interviewed in Washington worked outside the home and pooled their incomes with partners (if they were living with a man).[9] Every one of these women felt that their participation in the wage-labor force earned them the right to voice opinions when decisions about expenditures and other household issues arose. Half of the women were single mothers or single women without children and therefore did not encounter conflicts about gender roles within their households. Half of those who were married (or living with a man) met their partners in the United States and formulated or negotiated their roles on their own terms within this "first-world" culture. The women in this group reported that their partners in the United States willingly helped with housework on a regular basis.

In only one household was a man responsible for all of the housecleaning chores, while his wife did most of the cooking and grocery shopping. More commonly, housekeeping and cooking responsibilities were shared equally by both partners—particularly in households where women held full-time white-collar jobs outside the home (e.g., as counselors, teachers, or secretaries). In several households men did most of the cooking, while women were responsible for the cleaning. In the few cases where men held two or more jobs, women said that they did not ask their partners to share the housework. Only two women among all those interviewed retained the belief that home was the woman's domain and that it was their responsibility as women to take care of their husbands. Most women—single, married, or accompanied—believed in principle that men should share household chores if both partners worked full-time outside the home.

Few Central American men had been accustomed to sharing household responsibilities and child care in their countries of origin, and half of the married or accompanied men interviewed in Washington continued to balk at doing so after settling in the United States. Even when women worked full-time outside the home, these men still expected their partners to do most of the cooking, cleaning, and caring for children in the household. One woman (Eva) who worked at a social service agency insisted that men "don't even pick up the dishes when they finish eating! With all my friends and family, the men expect women to do all the work. When they live alone, men learn to do the dishes and laundry themselves but once they get married, they expect women to do everything." Yet Eva herself was able to negotiate an equal sharing of household chores and child care with her U.S.-born husband. She believed that only women who formed new attachments to men after they migrated to the United States might be successful in convincing men to share domestic responsibilities and child care. Teresa Lopez was a prime example of this type of relationship, since she had recently allowed her boyfriend to move into the apartment she shared with her son. She proudly relished her authority within her household as she opined: "Men are very different here. In the United States I can insist that my *compañero* [partner] help me with the housework, and I know many marriages where the women make men do more housework in this country. In El Salvador, all the women have to do whatever men tell them to do, but not in the United States!" Nonetheless, other women complained that men from their countries of origin still displayed patriarchal attitudes toward women even after they migrated and settled in the United States.

Such perceptions may be indicative of a sea change in women's expectations and personal goals once they become adjusted to North American culture and work routines. These changes are far more dramatic and prompt than those exhibited by their male compatriots.

One consequence of women's greater financial independence and adoption of new cultural norms in the United States is that they are less likely to tolerate physical abuse from a partner as they gain confidence in their abilities to support themselves. Women also say that men are less likely to abuse them physically (and children as well), because there are more societal sanctions against domestic violence in the United States. Carmen Montes, for example, confided that her husband developed an alcohol problem after a long period of unemployment in the United States. When he became intoxicated one night and tried to hit her, she threatened to call the police and actually picked up the phone in order to place the call. Her husband immediately backed off and never physically threatened her after that time. Carmen felt that her life had improved immeasurably since she settled in the United States. She claimed that

> Women in my country are like slaves to their husbands, even when they earn money by working and most women do work. It is much more acceptable for men to abuse women in El Salvador. My *compañero* used to beat me when we lived there but since we came to the United States, I don't allow him to do it anymore. At least women can find protection here.

But Rhina Garcia and Marina Suarez asserted that among the families they counseled, men still treated women badly in the United States if the men had been accustomed to such behavior in their countries of origin. Rhina (the nurse from Guatemala) explained: "Men demand more of women than they did at home, where women didn't have to work as hard. Now women have to do many jobs [inside and outside the home]. The men from El

Salvador especially are taught to be very macho and there is a lot of domestic violence in these families." Likewise, Marina felt that the potential for domestic violence within Central American families might increase upon settlement in the United States because people, particularly men who were unable to maintain steady employment, found drugs and alcohol more accessible when they became depressed. Althea, a preschool teacher, believed that if men physically abused their wives and children at home, they were unlikely to stop the practice when they moved to the United States. "I often see children coming to our school with bruises on them, and I know many men act violently towards their wives and children here."

Most women asserted that relationships became more complicated and contentious as women tried to relate to men under altered circumstances in their adopted country. Maria Herrera, for example, was raised in El Salvador until she entered high school in the United States, and she observed that "men's behavior changes because they have to learn to follow different cultural rules, to see and accept many things when both partners work and scrape to make a living. Women have very different roles here and the men have to adjust to them." Another young woman lambasted the men from her country as macho traditionalists but later admitted that she had succeeded in convincing her Salvadoran father to allow her to live with her boyfriend in Washington.

When women initiate changes in gender roles within a "first-world" culture—for example, by dressing like North Americans and working away from home all day—the reaction from men is often negative. Several informants claimed that their marriages broke up because husbands became jealous after they began working outside the home. Carmen confessed that her husband was exceedingly jealous of her newfound independence and resented the long hours she spent on her job away from home. "He thinks I'm looking for another man because I like to go to work so much!" Particularly if wives work when their husbands are unemployed, men feel threatened as their wives exhibit greater financial and personal independence. The strain on families occasionally leads to divorce, especially in the early years after migration to the United States. Families in which the husband or wife migrated alone in advance of the partner are particularly vulnerable to the stresses of resettlement in the United States. Marina Suarez observed that "if the man comes first and leaves his wife and children at home, he usually finds another woman here. There is this idea that men from El Salvador have that they can't be alone for a long time and they need a woman. A lot of women accept this and think it's okay. Even if the woman comes to the United States first, when the man is left behind he makes another family there." Rhina Garcia, who counseled many pregnant women in her social service agency, noted that most of the women who frequented her agency were separated from their partners and children because the women migrated to the United States first. She related the story of one of her clients, a woman who left six children and her partner in El Salvador to search for work in Washington. When the woman learned that her husband had been killed in the fighting in El Salvador, she grew lonely and despondent. Almost immediately she met another man and became pregnant by him. "Most of the women who come to our agency admit that they got pregnant because they were lonely. They don't speak English when they come here and they don't know about clinics where they can get help with family planning."

Settlement in the United States and the ensuing cultural contradictions and tensions are magnified for the children of recent immigrants. Parents are unable to mediate as children attempt to find their niche in a new society, particularly when the parents are forced to work long hours away from home or are compelled to separate because of domestic problems. Alienation within the family increases with time as children become acculturated more quickly than their parents and lose respect for parental authority. Young people come of age as obvious outsiders seeking to belong in a city known for its high crime rate and drug wars as well as its racial tensions. In the process of becoming "Americanized," trying to be like their peers, or even trying to help the family with extra income, immigrant youths may be sorely tempted by the easy money and fast life of drug dealing. They may also join street gangs, which confer a sense of safety and belonging.[10]

For those who fled their countries because of political persecution or because they were unable to provide a living for their families, migration becomes a Catch 22 situation. Individuals move north in order to help maintain the family back home or to ensure their safety by relocating family members to the United States; but the separations and cultural distances they must traverse enhance the loneliness that causes some to look for new partners, peers, or gangs upon resettlement. Families are torn apart amid the contradictions and struggles surrounding them, and unexpected outcomes may be worse than the problems that inspired the migration in the first place. As Rhina wryly observed: "That's the worst part about coming to America and it's the thing that's affecting our societies the most—that families break up when someone comes to America. The children never behave as well when they come here and easily get into trouble with drugs because of the disintegration of the family."

Freedom or Nothing Left to Lose?

The levels at which women experience personal freedom and autonomy in the United States depend fundamentally on such factors as marital status, urban versus rural origin, education level, and other indicators of class background. The consensus among all the Central American women interviewed in Washington is that women enjoy more independence and freedom in the United States than they had in their countries of origin; but they pay dearly for these rights by having to work harder than they did at home, often at jobs below their skill levels, and by having to juggle full-time work with added family responsibilities. Regardless of class background and marital status, most women insisted that they enjoyed more rights in their marriages after migration to this country, rights that came with full-time jobs, economic independence, and greater control over financial resources. Only one woman in the interview sample was completely financially dependent on her partner, and she was so because he refused to allow her to work outside the home when she came to the United States. After five years of virtual seclusion with her children in their small apartment, Marta ascribed women's freedom in the United States above all to economic independence. "If a man is supporting a woman he still thinks he has more rights over her and she has no freedom or economic security."[11]

Women with lower levels of education emphasized that they had less control over financial resources when they were living in their countries of origin. Teresa Lopez, who grew up in a rural town in El Salvador and only finished three years of formal education, commented: "Since I came here I was able to develop myself because I can work and go to school and make my own decisions about where I go or what I do. In my country many women have to stay home and they can't work or have their own money. I am glad that women don't need men here and they can live better without them."

Many women applaud the fact that hard work in the United States enables them to earn and spend their own money as they please—at stores, in restaurants, or socializing with friends. They appreciate such forms of independence as owning cars and literally wearing pants (trousers) in the family (a practice that is taboo in many settings in Central America). Women's economic independence accompanies widening social and personal opportunities that were lacking in their countries of origin. Patricia, a divorced mother of two children with seven years of education, believed that in the United States "if you want to be somebody you can do it. Even if I am old, if I want to study I can do it. In my country, even if you work, the pay is not that good and you can only manage to buy food and that's it. But here, if you work really hard and you want to buy a new car, you can do it." The ultimate freedom for many of these women is the option of leaving living situations in which partners physically abuse them. Carmen, whose unemployed husband had abused her, was the sole supporter of a family of seven. The fact that she controlled her own money and drove her own car had obviously empowered her, although she complained that life in the United States was difficult and that she often felt beleaguered by pressures that were nonexistent in El Salvador.

Teresa Lopez believed that women were not really "free" in this country, because they had to work longer hours with higher stress levels in the United States. "I wasn't really free until six years ago when I finally had some savings and could buy a new car. For almost ten years I had to live and work in other people's houses and I wasn't free," she lamented. Once they earned their independence and became accustomed to newfound freedoms, women like Teresa expressed profound gratitude for enhanced economic independence and the opportunity it afforded them to control their own destinies. In particular, the women who originated in rural sectors of their countries and had little formal education relished the opportunity to work outside the home in the United States. Many of these women were expected to work in the home or fields in their countries of origin and held little control over personal or financial decisions. For rural women who adapted to life in the United States and exercised the freedom to venture out on their own, the resulting conflicts with men were far more stressful than for their compatriots from urban areas. Immigrant men with little formal education and of rural origin tended to exhibit greater difficulties in adjusting to partners who had achieved financial independence. In the social service agency where she worked, Marina had seen families break apart because "it's not easy to change the minds and habits that people have had for many years, and it causes problems for couples." On the other hand, well-educated women who came from the middle and upper classes in their countries of origin but who experienced downward mobility in their careers upon migration were less enthusiastic about the benefits that migration conferred upon women—particularly if they were forced to migrate for political reasons.

Additionally, marital status influenced women's assessment of the personal gains they had realized upon migration to the United States. Married women said that in the United States they had to work harder to keep up with the physical and emotional needs of their families, which left them little time to enjoy enhanced independence. Consuela, a divorced mother of two, asserted that "women are more free here in every way, especially in being able to work and drive cars. But it's better for single women because married women have so many responsibilities that they don't have much time to enjoy their independence." Married women complained that after they migrated to the United States, their work load doubled if they had to work full-time inside and outside the home without the help of extended family. Carmen lamented: "Only the men are going to be able to better themselves financially in this country. Women can barely make ends meet . . . it isn't freedom to be isolated and alienated in this culture here."

Several married women vocalized a deep-seated envy of single women, since they held the impression that single women were able to venture out when they pleased, to work for good wages, and then to spend the money on themselves—to a degree unprecedented in their countries of origin. Some of the single women verified that they did indeed enjoy added personal liberties as a consequence of their labor force participation and the acquisition of possessions such as automobiles. Even more so they relished the freedom from community pressures and sanctions that were an integral part of life in small Central American towns. As Isabel noted, "In El Salvador women are rejected for doing 'bad' things. But people can't fire you for your personal behavior here. Women can go out with more than one man and they are free to do what they want . . . even abortion is an option here, which it isn't in El Salvador." Other women observed that single women had the unprecedented liberty to date different men, to live alone, or to live with a man without being criticized by the surrounding community. "A woman never really has the ability to experience what it is to live on her own in our countries," according to Eva. "Women have more sexual freedom in the United States and they can drink and do anything that men do, which is impossible in our countries."

Several women observed that too much sexual freedom was harmful and that as recent immigrants they were more vulnerable to isolation and loneliness after they settled in the United States. Althea, a college-educated teacher, commented that although many families boasted of improvements in financial status and material acquisitions in the United States, they faced more alienation and greater challenges to the moral fabric of their relationships. "People get confused because they have so many things to divert and entertain themselves with here—the bars and restaurants, for example—and they think that this is freedom." Compared with what they left behind in their countries of origin, immigrants confront the rigors of life in the United States with less time to unwind and socialize among families and friends. Especially for parents, anxieties are amplified because of the profusion of unfamiliar influences on their children and the underlying racial tensions pervading American society. Without the ameliorating presence of extended families to help diffuse these pressures, parents are expected to be involved in the emotional lives of their children, to visit their schools, and to help children with problems they encounter in the United

States. Counseling children and assisting them with complex problems and influences within a foreign culture occupies a great deal of parents' time and resources.

Dreaming North American Dreams

Common themes repeatedly surfaced in the dreams that Central American women from a broad spectrum of backgrounds had formulated for themselves and for their families. They included home ownership, the prospect of better jobs, and furthering their individual development. After they had settled in the United States, most women generally associated the proverbial American dream with higher education. Over half of the women interviewed envisaged college or graduate school for their children, and three-fourths of them resolved to take classes and to acquire new skills themselves in the United States. Many expressed the desire to attend school to learn skills that could put them on more promising career paths. In particular, the women who came to the United States with high school degrees aspired to work as secretaries one day, and they resolved to learn English and word processing in order to surmount the frustrations they experienced in low-status domestic service jobs. An overwhelming majority of the women interviewed contemplated the future with optimism because they believed it was possible to develop themselves and to enable their children to attain high education levels in the United States.

Women with only a moderate level of education (six to ten years) formulated goals in line with the skill levels they brought with them from their countries of origin. Rosaria Lopez, the seamstress and former factory worker, aspired to operate her own dress-making shop someday; and another woman who cooked in a Mexican restaurant hoped to manage her own small restaurant in the future. Many women who held college degrees when they emigrated aspired to regain careers they once held or to assist and counsel people from their countries of origin. Two women voiced a desire to teach again, three social workers intended to pursue graduate degrees, and two counselors hoped to earn more money in order to buy their own homes someday. Whether women had only three years of education or held college degrees, all concurred in their aspirations for their children: they wanted their children to have the opportunity to attend college and to attain professional careers in the United States. Women like Patricia, who had experienced sharp downward mobility upon migration to the United States, intended to remain in this country specifically to further their children's education. "I'm working very hard because I want my children to be somebody. I don't want them to have to work at a Roy Rogers or clean other people's houses."

None of the women spoke of their tenure on jobs outside their homes as temporary. None of them expressed the desire to leave the wage-labor force in order to remain at home or to allow their partners to be sole supporters in the household. All the women said that they preferred to be busy and to work with other people on a job site in order to maintain their financial independence from men. Yet there were disturbing trade-offs for mothers who worked outside the home. Maria Herrera, the Salvadoran woman who earned the highest salary among the women in the interview sample, expressed the conflicts that her ambitions aroused.

> I've already reached many of my goals but at the expense of having to leave my children when they were little to work full-time. I would have preferred to be a full-time mother for awhile . . . I wasn't able to be with my children enough because my husband and I had to work full-time. Now I want my children to go to college and have some skills so that they can be in command of their job opportunities and not be dependent on anyone.

Few women still harbored intentions of returning to live in their countries of origin someday, although half of them admitted that they had only intended to live and work in the United States for two or three years when they first emigrated. Over time a third of the women had revised their plans and intended to reside permanently in the United States, and another third planned to retire someday in their countries of origin. Only one-fourth of the women still hoped to return to their countries of birth when "the situation improved," meaning peaceful living conditions and job opportunities.[12] Five years after the initial interviews, I spoke with many of these women again, and only two women out of twenty-two had actually returned to their countries of origin. Several women from El Salvador explained that although the government and insurgents had formally signed a peace treaty, conditions there remained tense and the peace tenuous. One of the women who returned to El Salvador did so because her husband had been elected to the new Congress of Deputies. But upon her return she was so alarmed at the extent of the violence in the country that she promptly sent two more sons and a daughter to join her daughters already living in the United States. Eva confessed that she remained in the United States because "the message I hear from everyone is 'do not come back here, because the country is not ready to receive you yet.'" Consuela contended that she must remain in the Washington area for the sake of her children. "It's not war any more in El Salvador, but it's not peace yet either. It's still not easy to live there, and there is too much robbery and violence. We don't have our beautiful country back yet."

Over time and with increasing exposure to North American norms and values, Central American men were also adapting to the transformations in gender roles that settlement in the United States conferred. Few men envisioned a return to their countries of origin as a means for regaining authority and privileges. Yet there were some who did return after agonizing at length over the relative merits of attempting to achieve success in a competitive "first-world" society. Eric Romero and his wife Silvia, for example, returned to Guatemala after spending two difficult years in the United States. Before their original migration Eric and Silvia had been working in relatively high-status jobs at a bank in Guatemala City. But when violence in Guatemala prevented them from living and working in peace, they decided to join Eric's parents and brothers in the United States. During their first year in Washington, Silvia worked as a housekeeper, while Eric worked as a dishwasher in a restaurant. He eventually found a better job as a warehouse manager, but when Silvia had a child and quit her job, they found that they could not survive on one salary. Eric had to take a second job at a commercial cleaning company and was unable to see his family even on weekends or evenings. Silvia became disillusioned with their lives in the United States and decided to return to Guatemala with the child. Eric followed her two months later, when he realized, "In the United States I will always be stuck in low-status jobs and will never be free from worries about making enough money for my family." Although Eric's parents and brothers obtained permanent-residence status, he claimed he never wanted to live in the United States again. "Why should I have to suffer in three jobs with low status just so my children can have some benefits when they grow up? I never could be with my children in the U.S., and parents and children have a different relationship there."

Two women had vowed in the initial interviews that they would return to their countries of origin someday because they believed that life was safer and healthier for children in a drug-free environment and with extensive family support systems surrounding them. Both women had actually left daughters behind to be raised by their grandmothers in Guatemala because, as one explained, "I wanted her to live with the love of God and of brothers and sisters around her without any discrimination. Even though we are poor in our country, it is better for children to grow up in an environment of love and support where life is more modest and sincere." The other woman planned to work hard for two or three years in order to return to El Salvador with money for her daughter's future. But five years later both women had remarried men from their countries of origin who were also living in Washington, and they had started new families in that city. Despite contradictory impulses to return home, newcomers often develop ineradicable ties over time to the communities where they live and work in the United States. Clearly these forces counterbalance those encouraging return to the country of origin, as Leo Chavez observed.[13] Experiences such as maintaining steady employment, learning English, forming a family in the United States, raising children in U.S. schools, adapting to North American culture, and ultimately gaining legal status lead inexorably to immigrant incorporation into U.S. society.

Eight

Conclusion

Somehow within a single generation, Washington, D.C., managed to attract entire villages, households, and extended families from El Salvador and other Central American countries, to the point that it could claim the second largest Salvadoran community and the third largest settlement of Central Americans in the United States. In many ways this migration constitutes a departure from the labor migrations of other Latin Americans to the United State, and the Central American immigrants who chose to settle in Washington may be embraced as "new immigrants."[1] Their settlement patterns were profoundly influenced by the fact that women predominated in the initial phase of the migration, by the distinctive gender differences that emerged in labor force participation patterns, and through the assumption of transformed gender roles.

A historical-structural framework was employed here to explain the origins and directionality of this Central American migration, along with certain facets of the labor market experiences of men and women. Labor recruitment theory also contributed to an understanding of the timing and composition of the migration. But since gendered labor recruitment was primarily responsible for determining the peculiar direction and gender composition of this particular migration, a focus on gender is essential in any analysis of the migration, settlement, and labor force participation patterns of recent Central American immigrants in the United States.

Gender Factors in the Migration Process

El Salvador serves as a prime example of a country where the forces that propel or cause migrations cannot be separated and neatly compartmentalized as political or economic in nature. The most densely populated mainland country in the Western Hemisphere, El Salvador was a battleground for access to land throughout the twentieth century as more and more land became concentrated in the hands of fewer and fewer families. Earlier studies demonstrated that three-fourths of all emigrants from El Salvador in the 1950s and 1960s came from the excluded population of landless or land-poor peoples, but no studies underlined the gender composition of these movements. To a large extent political-economic transformations—for example, the concentration of land in the hands of wealthy families and the increasing polarization, political repression, and violence in the societies—were occurring simultaneously in Guatemala, in Nicaragua, and (to a lesser extent) in Honduras. In all of these Central American countries, people migrated in response to economic dislocations and changes in the world economy and as a result of war and political persecution.

Women have predominated in migrations from rural to urban areas throughout most of Latin America for a number of years. But beginning in the 1960s Central American women pioneered and dominated the early labor migration to a distant city in the United States—that is, to Washington, D.C. Structural links between the United States and the Central American countries had expanded rapidly since the early 1960s on account of U.S. business, government, and cultural influences. Potential emigrants in Central American countries increasingly were made aware of conditions in the United States through burgeoning communication links (e.g., through radio and television, through consumer goods, and through the medium of social networks). When landless and land-poor peasants who were leaving El Salvador (and other Central American countries) were joined by students and teachers, by workers without jobs, by individuals who were persecuted or targeted for assassination, and by apolitical people who were caught between warring factions, many already had information about or close ties with cities in the United States because of the women who had migrated earlier for work.

The structural conditions that generate emigration from certain countries tend to be gender-specific, especially when linked with cultural norms and ideologies in both sending and receiving countries. In the case of El Salvador, these gender-based structural conditions had a profound impact on women: the nonexistence of paid work for women in rural areas; family traditions of encouraging daughters to depart; low marriage rates along with high rates of female-headed households; the not uncommon pattern where men may have multiple partners and may be linked loosely to several households; and the availability of domestic-service jobs in cities that attracted women with few employment opportunities in rural areas. Similarly, characteristics of labor markets in certain receiving cities may hold more allure for women than for men among those who wish to emigrate. Cultural norms also determine whether women or men are preferred as candidates for certain jobs, particularly in gender-segregated labor markets such as Washington, D.C., with its overabundance of service-sector jobs. The exodus of U.S.-born women out of such gender-stereotyped occupations as domestic service and child care since the 1960s and the increasing demand for low-wage workers to fill these jobs obviously presented more attractive employment opportunities to Central American women than to men.

Because of a high proportion of female-headed households in countries such as El Salvador, women who wished to emigrate were the primary actors in decisions about when and where they desired to move. A majority of the women who converged on Washington in the 1960s and 1970s did so as single individuals or as single mothers and heads of households who sought ways to provide for their families, and most of them emigrated without the approval or assistance of men. Gendered labor recruitment was responsible for luring many of these early immigrants to Washington. The testimonies of women like Rosa Lopez, Lucia Herrera, and Rhina Garcia illustrate how over the years Washington's government, diplomatic, and professional workforce recruited immigrants (particularly women) who could furnish basic services as domestic workers and child-care providers.

A constellation of forces prompted the shift from employer-induced to family- or network-based migration in the movement of Central Americans to Washington, D.C. At the same time, the migration pattern shifted from one in which women predominated to a more general movement of men and women. Washington was never a major center of manufacturing, assembly, or production work, and the city did not experience an abrupt shift from a goods-producing to a service-based economy. Instead, its transformation can be attributed primarily to population growth, diversification (i.e., the increase of biotechnology, defense, and research-and-development firms), and gentrification rather than to structural change. The city's phenomenal growth since 1960 resulted in the proliferation of highly skilled jobs, as well as an expansion of low-skilled and service jobs.

An international capital and new "world city," Washington posed an attractive destination for new immigrants, and this attraction was enhanced by the vibrant economic conditions persisting throughout the 1980s. Throughout most of that decade, Washington had the highest average household income of any major metropolitan area in the country, as well as the nation's highest proportion of women in the workforce (69 percent). The city has perpetually suffered from an acute shortage of day-care facilities and a commensurate abundance of high-income families who can afford to procure housekeeping and child-care services. These professionals eagerly sought or recruited the services of domestic workers and child-care providers from other countries to relieve them of day-care and household responsibilities. They also created a demand for the products made and sold by growing numbers of specialty shops (e.g., gourmet foods and fine linen), all of which depended on semiskilled and unskilled workers. A persistent dearth of North Americans to fill low-wage jobs in the Washington area led to a minuscule unemployment figure of 2.9 percent for the region in 1988. Leverage in wages was possible for Central American immigrants, particularly those with documents, because of the tight labor market conditions that persisted throughout the Washington metropolitan area.

These noteworthy features, then, distinguish the migration of Central Americans to Washington from similar movements of Mexicans, Dominicans, and other Latin Americans to major cities in the United States. As primary actors in the decision-making stages, women initiated the migration and pioneered the movement to a city that did not have a well-established Latin American community ready to receive and assist them with support services. Many of the women were recruited to work or had jobs arranged for them in Washington by diplomatic or professional families. Distinct gender differences emerged in the settlement patterns that ensued as a result of a gendered labor migration. Central American women brought more family members along with them (or sent for them in time) than Central American men did, which led to a relatively stable, legal, and permanent immigration. In addition, women had to form their own social networks, which eventually provided job referrals, housing, and other forms of assistance to later arrivals from their countries of origin. As Nestor Rodriguez has observed, women's presence contributes to the rapid development of a thriving community that ensures the continuation of cultural traditions and assists coethnics in the settlement process. Women immigrants "fuel the development of families and, hence, of family-related activities, such as weddings and baptisms, that trigger community social participation."[2]

One final distinction between Central American migration patterns and those of other Latin American migrations is the fact that a substantial proportion of the immigrants were forced to leave their homes because of civil wars and political repression. Many émigrés were highly educated white-collar and professional people who brought their skills and talents to the labor pools of U.S. cities without posing as a burden on public resources. Yet the overwhelming majority of immigrants from Central American countries were not recognized as political refugees and encountered a hostile reception by the U.S. government upon arrival in this country. Consequently, family members, social networks, and social service agencies (largely staffed by women) had to mediate for those in need of food, housing, job referrals, and training. Gender-based networks were often the only conduit to safe havens and sanctuaries for later immigrants who fled their countries as a result of political persecution and war in the 1980s. Indeed, networks grew to such an extent that half of the later immigrants from Central American countries chose to go to Washington because they had a family member in that city, and many others went because they heard that there were more jobs and higher wages in Washington than elsewhere in the country. Very few were left to find jobs and housing on their own, without the advice or assistance of seasoned compatriots.

Labor Force Participation Patterns

From a study of this nature, questions arise about the intrinsic character of gender-based social networks and how they vary when women predominate in a migration. Even larger questions emerge with the striking gender differences in the labor market experiences of Central American men and women: with regard to labor market insertion patterns, wage levels, occupational mobility, and the range of occupations open to immigrant women as opposed to immigrant men. The large disparity in wages and job mobility for Central American immigrants can hardly be attributed to human capital differences between men and women or to any deficiencies on the part of the women. By all human capital measures, Central American women held distinct advantages over men—that is, in length of time in the United States, in level of education, in English-speaking ability, and legal status. Even when comparing social capital, women exhibited stronger ties to social networks and profited from them to a greater extent than men. But the sector of employment in which men worked was more important than any of their background characteristics in determining wage levels and job mobility, and structural factors were clearly in their favor. Central American men found unusually advantageous employment opportunities in the Washington area. A booming construction industry and tight labor market conditions throughout the 1980s translated into higher wages than comparable jobs paid in other cities, regardless of education levels, English proficiency, and legal status. The proportion of the Central American men surveyed in Washington who were employed in construction was far higher (at 61 percent) than the figures for Latin American men in other U.S. cities (such as Mexicans in California, at 18 percent), and wages far surpassed those recorded for Mexican men in California as well as for Central American men in Houston.[3]

Central American women experienced less economic "success" and occupational mobility than Central American men in the Washington area labor market despite their human capital advantages and extensive use of social networks. Women exhibited little mobility in wage levels or job status largely because of structural factors, that is, the narrow range of occupations open to them and the fact that they were confined to informal or secondary-sector jobs. For immigrant women with lower levels of education, domestic service is hardly "transitional work," since they will probably never experience mobility out of the occupation. Domestic service is an occupation with built-in idiosyncracies that bar women from career advancement and wage mobility to an extent that men never experience in the occupational sectors that they dominate. Women in domestic service work in isolation from compatriots; they are insulated from more diverse networks with information on other types of jobs; and they lack the opportunities to learn new job skills (such as word processing or administrative skills). Most domestic workers are unable to organize themselves into unions and thus have no means for redressing grievances or improving work conditions. These circumstances are especially acute for live-in domestic workers, and most of them seek to make the transition to live-out domestic work as early as possible. Few other occupations entail such enormous responsibility (for the lives of children and the welfare of homes) and yet are so poorly remunerated and devoid of vital benefits such as medical and retirement insurance, sick leave, and paid vacations.

A rigid sex-typing of jobs may occur among immigrant women anywhere in the United States as soon as they enter the labor market. But in a service-oriented city such as Washington, semiskilled women who would most likely move into production-and-assembly jobs in other urban areas in the United States find few opportunities for employment outside of domestic service. Most white-collar jobs are out of reach for Central American women because such jobs generally require fluency in English, higher education levels, and the possession of legal documents. The few women who were able to move into pink- or white-collar jobs (e.g., in secretarial, teaching, and counseling positions) attained higher status but not necessarily higher-paid employment than their counterparts in domestic service. Employment stagnation and wage discrimination are indeed problems for women nationally, regardless of their origins. Several studies have noted that women of all national origins, Anglo and other U.S.-born women included, attain far lower proportions of upper-income job categories (in professional and managerial positions) than men do.[4] They stress that the occupational segregation by gender and the triple role that women have to assume as wives, mothers, and wage workers probably account for the fact that human capital variables make little difference in women's earnings.

Gender factors clearly emerge as preeminent in the analysis of immigrant labor market incorporation and render structural and personal characteristics inadequate as explanations for the performance of Central American immigrants in Washington's labor market. Long-term patterns of economic adaptation for Central American men and women are as yet impossible to determine because they are relatively recent immigrants and because their experiences vary widely with the divergent labor markets in different cities. The question that must be answered in time and with further research is whether first-generation immigrant women with high levels of human capital eventually achieve marked improvement in wages and employment mobility, or whether occupational advancement and career opportunities become available only to the generations that succeed them.

Another issue that further research must address is how new immigration laws affect immigrant women as opposed to immigrant men and to what extent U.S. immigration laws (IRCA in particular) convey an unintended gender bias. Interviews with employers, trade union officials, social service agency representatives, and Central American families revealed that IRCA has had little lasting effect on labor market conditions for recent immigrants in Washington. IRCA's employer sanctions provision affected small, ethnically-owned, and competitive businesses (e.g., in the secondary sector) to the extent that they reported more difficulty in finding documented workers than did larger, more stable firms that paid higher wages. Most employers admitted that they complied with the letter but not with the spirit of the law. Undocumented immigrant men initially experienced greater difficulties securing stable jobs than undocumented women did, but most men were eventually able to locate or purchase documents that satisfied the requirements of employers. More men than women claimed that they were fired from jobs as a result of IRCA, lending credence to the supposition that domestic service insulates women from IRCA's effects; few private-household employers demanded to see legal documents from immigrant workers (especially women). Transformations in local economies, tight labor market conditions, and economic recessions have a more pervasive influence on immigrant workers overall, whether documented or undocumented.

Problems associated with legal status, which were magnified with the passage of IRCA, may keep needier new immigrants away from social service agencies, since these agencies are barred by law from offering job assistance to individuals without legal documents. One director of a social service agency maintained that IRCA had a considerable negative impact on families in the Central American community. "It's much more difficult to find jobs for people now, there's less security for them when they find work, and the employers who take workers on a contract basis can exploit them more easily." She added that the use of alcohol and drugs in immigrant communities had increased dramatically in the years since IRCA went into effect, and that more Latin American youths were becoming involved in drug markets. But housing problems and the high cost of living in Washington may have an even greater impact on the Latin American community than IRCA did. As one counselor observed, "People can still find work, but not enough to pay the bills. Even if someone is documented and making $5.50 an hour, they can't afford to live here and support a family." Differences in how new immigration laws impact women as opposed to how they impact men, and how these laws complicate the tenuous paths toward economic survival and cultural adaptation for new immigrants, are issues that have not been adequately addressed in the literature as yet.

Self-Concepts and Gender Roles

A final area in which Central American immigrants distinguish themselves as "new immigrants" is in the reformulation of gender roles upon settlement in the United States. Many Central American women made the decision to emigrate and actually moved to a distant U.S. city of their own accord and by their own resources, especially if they had jobs arranged for them in the United States. Women who made such decisions and accomplished the arduous move to the United States on their own had already embarked upon a process of transformation in self-perception and gender roles. These immigrants reveal that gender roles are perpetually in a state of flux during the migration and settlement processes and that as a result their relationships are fraught with contradictions. The process of migration and re-settlement alters gender roles to an enormous extent, and a majority of Central American women maintain that they enjoy more personal independence and autonomy in the United States, particularly if they work for wages. But the flip side of the coin is that women have to work much harder than they did at home and that job-related stresses often take a heavy toll on their personal and family lives.

The degree of contentment that Central American women expressed over their lives in the United States depended largely upon whether they experienced a sharp decline in social and occupational status upon migration and whether they had any hope of mobility out of low-status jobs. After several years of work in domestic service, for example, the women who had moved into higher-status jobs as secretaries, teachers, and counselors voiced contentment with their achievements in the United States even though their salaries were far from adequate. Similarly, women with low education levels who held few aspirations to shift out of domestic service expressed a certain satisfaction with their work and personal lives in this country. Most of these women were appreciative of their jobs and glad to be working for "decent" wages. But the women who had experienced an irreversible decline in job status and could find no alternative to jobs in domestic service in the Washington area (generally semi-skilled workers who had worked in factories or stores in their countries of origin) displayed a sullen discontentment with their working lives. Most of these women worked hard because they wanted their children to have the opportunity for higher education and the higher status careers that have eluded them.

Other problems in the settlement process that created hardships for both men and women were discrimination from landlords, employers, and neighbors; the language barrier (if they were unable to speak English); the new immigration law, which complicated the search for stable employment for people who were undocumented; and unemployment or unstable work conditions, particularly for undocumented Central American men. Dealing with discrimination and exploitation by employers or other Americans was an intransigent problem for both immigrant men and women when they settled in the United States. Coming from more homogeneous societies in Central American countries (such as El Salvador), few of those interviewed had experienced the depth of racial or ethnic enmity and discrimination that they encountered in the United States. Isabel Martinez remarked at how deeply she felt the divisions in U.S. society between black, brown, and white people. She feared for her children because they were often subject to nasty forms of discrimination. "Sometimes I feel like a cockroach crawling on the ground because of the way people treat me. And my daughter comes home from school and tells me that other kids are saying things to her, and I feel bad." Such problems may enhance the sense of cultural isolation and low self-esteem that many immigrants must contend with, particularly if they are locked into servile work that is far below their levels of education and expertise.

Most Central American women worked outside the home to contribute to the household's sustenance and as a result they became empowered in their roles as major providers. The extent to which women gained personal freedom, independence, and a sense that they were living more rewarding lives after migrating to the United States often hinged upon personal characteristics such as marital status, education level, socioeconomic background, and urban versus rural origin. But all women who earned wages were able to use that financial independence as a vehicle for gaining control over other areas of their lives, for negotiating more equitable sharing of household responsibilities, and for demanding greater autonomy. They believed that they had earned the right to go where they pleased, to take classes and "develop" themselves, to purchase their own cars, to socialize with friends, and to participate in decisions about household expenditures.

Married and single women alike complained that men changed little in their roles and attitudes toward women after migrating to the United States, and that as a result relationships became more complicated and contentious upon resettlement here. The stresses of working long hours at low-wage service jobs, of adjusting to a strange culture and altered roles within the family, and of dealing with problems related to legal status are often severe enough to cause the break-up of marriages. Even though migration may enable women to augment their independence and power within the family, "the success of the migration project may hinge on the maintenance of household structures that permit the pooling of several rather low incomes. . . . If the newfound autonomy of employed immigrant women leads to marital disruption rather than altered power relations in the traditional household, the collective mobility project is likely to fail, leading to poverty . . . in the United States," as Sherri Grasmuck and Patricia Pessar (1991:202) observed. Only with time will the actual dimensions of the personal toll that migration entails become clear.

The immigration experience obviously holds different benefits for women and men. Migration and resettlement in the United

States has enabled a sizable proportion of women to shirk traditional roles and patterns of dependence so that they may realize aspirations for financial independence, enhanced autonomy, and personal goals for their children.[5] In certain senses they have achieved more than Central American men, who must relinquish some of the privileges of patriarchal cultures. Yet women confront more barriers than men in their pursuit of personal development and career advancement in the United States, particularly in cities such as Washington that are replete with genderstereotyped jobs from which women may never escape. For both men and women, migration indeed entails a melange of bitter blessings.

Epilogue

What has become of the Central American women and men who spoke so eloquently about their journeys to Washington and about their experiences and expectations in the United States? Five years after the initial discussions with the women in the interview sample, I was able to locate or to learn news about twenty-two of the thirty women. Most had prospered after residing in the Washington area for almost ten years, while some had weathered taxing personal storms in their adjustments to a foreign (North) American culture.

The extensive Lopez family, for example, still gathered regularly for Sunday dinners at Teresa's apartment. The matriarch of the family, Rosa, and her husband, Javier, had both retired but continued to reside in the Washington area rather than return to El Salvador as they had once planned. Teresa had married her partner from Honduras (the father of her second child) and they still shared household duties in the same small apartment in Silver Spring, Maryland. She continued to clean houses by day and extracted an annual inflation stipend from her employers. In 1993 she commanded $60 per house for a five- or six-hour workday. Her husband worked for the construction company that employed him when he was undocumented, and he had since become a permanent resident through Teresa. Her cousin Rosaria (the former seamstress who was earning only $5 per hour at the time of the first interview) accepted a position with Amtrak and earned $8 an hour with full medical and vacation benefits. She and her husband, Manuel, had bought a house in a Maryland suburb and had had second child. Manuel had been laid off from his construction job in 1992 because of the recession, but as a permanent resident he was eligible to collect unemployment. Rosaria's mother returned to El Salvador after the peace agreement was signed, because her husband was elected to the Congress of Deputies. But the mother sent Rosaria's two brothers and sisters to the Washington area because the violence in that troubled country continued. Rosaria's sisters found employment as child-care providers for professional families in the Washington area (through Rosaria's or Teresa's networks), and her brothers worked in the wallpapering business.

Rosa Lopez's other niece, Eva, attended evening courses at a local college in order to complete her bachelor's degree (which was interrupted when her university was closed in El Salvador in the early 1980s). She worked by day for a national organization that provided assistance to Hispanic-origin students in public schools, and earned $21,000 annually (or $10 an hour). Her husband (a former job counselor at a social service agency) worked for a county government agency in Maryland, training welfare recipients for future employment; he earned $35,000 annually ($17 an hour). They, too, had bought a house in a Maryland suburb and had added a second child to the family. Eva had invited her parents to join her in the United States, and through her they were able to obtain permanent residency, since Eva was by then a U.S. citizen. Her brothers lived in the Washington area as well, but the brother with whom she had shared an apartment when she first moved to that city recently died of AIDS.

Eva's sister Marta, who was unemployed and estranged from

her husband at the time of the first interview, resided with him once again in their new home in Maryland. They had had a fourth child, and Marta (a former teacher) continued to work with the children at home. She attended English classes and a support group at a local social service agency and was waiting for a position to open up at a local day-care center, where she hoped to work and to place her children. Marta said she had regained her self-confidence partly because she was now able to communicate in English, and because she had joined an evangelical church and received a great deal of support and encouragement from the congregation.

Rhina Garcia, the social service agency counselor from Guatemala, was working at a medical clinic in Washington counseling Latin American women who required prenatal services. She earned a better salary than she had at the social service agency (about $12 per hour as opposed to $7) and was looking for a house to buy with her husband. Marina Suarez, the other social service agency counselor from El Salvador, worked at a prison counseling offenders of Latin American origin. She, too, had increased her earnings dramatically to $14 an hour (up from $9), and she had recently purchased a house in the Maryland suburbs as well. Her friend Althea (the former college teacher) still worked at the day-care center where she earned only $7 an hour, and she had not made much of an attempt to learn English. She said she had no ambition left because she felt old and tired, and she no longer planned to take the courses she would need in order to earn a license to teach in D.C. public schools. She and her husband had bought a house in Maryland, and their two daughters were attending college in the area.

Isabel Martinez spoke fluent English and still took great pride in practicing her second language. While she was working at a social service agency as a receptionist earning $6 an hour, she had taken a training course for health assistants. She now worked for another community agency as a "health promoter" (a type of physician's assistant) at $8 an hour. Her husband Luis was still working as a cook in a restaurant, but he had finally mustered the courage to ask for more money and was earning $8 an hour as well. Isabel and Luis planned to return to El Salvador or Guatemala when they retired because, in their words, "we won't have enough energy to work forever, and we can have a better life there without crime or high rents." They, too, had recently purchased a home in a Maryland suburb, and their two daughters had applied to colleges, seeking scholarships on the basis of their excellent academic records.

Sarai Nunez, who had a high school degree and yearned to work as a secretary someday, still worked at a downtown Washington hotel as a housekeeper (earning $9 an hour). Because she had a difficult pregnancy with her second child, she was forced to remain at home for seven months, and the hotel where she was employed allowed her to resume her position as a housekeeper when she was well enough to return. Sarai still hoped to be a secretary someday when she had the time to improve her English skills. She and her husband, who also worked at a hotel (but as a caterer), had obtained permanent residence status under the general-amnesty provision and had bought a house in the Maryland suburbs. She had been able to import her mother and sisters to the United States, and the mother baby-sat for Sarai's children while she was at work.

Jose Sandoval was able to retain his position as a drywall finisher at $16 an hour despite the recession that reverberated throughout the construction industry in the Washington area. His wife, Luisa, however, lost most of the houses she used to clean even though she and Jose were documented permanent residents. She blamed the recession and feared that she would have to look for a job with a commercial cleaning company in the near future. Nevertheless, she and Jose had also bought a house and were still planning to save enough money to return to El Salvador someday, where they hoped to purchase a small business.

The two sisters who were divorced mothers, Consuela and Patricia, had not fared as well as some of their compatriots. Patricia still cleaned houses by day, and she asked a $5 yearly increase in salary from each employer (per house per day), but she still had no medical insurance for herself or for her children. Once she and the children had obtained permanent residency, she was able to quit her second job with a commercial cleaning company. She was urging her children to apply to colleges, and she was receiving some child support from her former husband. Consuela received nothing from her former partner and was responsible for supporting two children and two grandchildren. Her daughter, Vilma, had dropped out of high school when she became pregnant with her first child, and two years later Vilma had a second child. Vilma had never held a paying job and did little to help her mother around the house with the two babies. She had recently moved out of her mother's apartment and had gone to live with a boyfriend, taking the younger of the two children along with her. Consuela's son had joined a street gang of Latin American youths and thus far had managed to stay out of jail even though neighbors had caught him driving a stolen car with his friends. Consuela had developed a serious drinking problem and had recently injured her back at the restaurant where she worked as a cook. She had no medical benefits and had been out of work for months. The green card that she attained through her employers had not helped her to improve her financial situation, and she worried about the future for her teenage son and grandchildren.

Two other single mothers, Anna Lopez and Blanca Diaz, had left small children in their countries of origin with the intention of returning home when they had compiled some savings in the United States (after two or three years). Both women had recently married fellow Salvadorans who also resided in Washington, and both had started new families in the United States. Neither Blanca nor Anna had seen their daughters in El Salvador again even though they continued to send money home for their support. Blanca had obtained permanent residence status through her employer (a commercial cleaning company), and

Anna had a green card because of the amnesty provision and continued to clean houses for private families. One other woman who worked as a live-in housekeeper for a diplomatic family, Julia Mendez, had left her employer's residence to share an apartment with a friend. Even though she was able to save money from her housekeeping work, she had spent all of it bringing three sisters to the United States from El Salvador. Now, she maintained, she must begin to save for herself as she cleaned houses for $60 a day. She had diligently attended English-language and word-processing classes, hoping to secure a secretarial job someday. One of her employers had applied for work certification for Julia, and she hoped to obtain her green card soon (she had come to the United States on a diplomatic visa because she worked for diplomats for seven years). One student who was attending graduate school in the Washington area had recently returned to El Salvador when she was unable to find a professional job in the United States after graduation.

Two of the women who were reinterviewed reported that husbands or partners had lost jobs (mainly in construction) because of the recession of the early 1990s, and as a result these women were forced to work harder in order to support their families. Only one woman said that she lost work (e.g., houses to clean) because of the recession. Yet with interest rates at an all-time low, fully half of the women who were reinterviewed (or close to one-third of all women in the interview sample) had cemented their ties to the Washington area by buying homes in the suburbs with partners or on their own. At least two-thirds of the women in the sample had also attained permanent-resident status, further sealing their bonds to their adopted country.[6] All of the women who had expressed a desire to buy a home in the Washington area had been able to do so, largely because of the low interest rates available to first-time home buyers during the recent recession. Many of the women who had aspired to improve themselves by attending English, word-processing, or computer-programming classes had embarked upon this course with great determination and energy, despite exhausting workdays with fulltime jobs and family responsibilities. Other women who had pinned their hopes on college careers for their children were overjoyed to be within sight of their goal.

Appendix:
Methodology

The data and life histories presented in this book were collected in detailed interviews and surveys conducted between 1988 and 1990. Fieldwork for the project involved a multimethod approach in order to complement survey data with ethnographic material. The work also draws upon my involvement—as a teacher of English and a volunteer worker in special projects—with several social service agencies that cater to Latin American immigrants. The project initially entailed interviews with thirty representatives of social service agencies, local government, and community-based groups working primarily with Central American immigrants. These visits aided in the identification of vital issues confronting Central American immigrants in the Washington area, in the collection of data on client populations, and in pinpointing streets and apartment complexes where a large number of recent immigrants from Central American countries resided. Later, as part of a project studying the impact of IRCA for a congressional report, I interviewed seventy-five employers in the construction, restaurant, and cleaning industries who employed a significant number of immigrants of Central American origin. These interviews assessed the labor market trends and changes in the workplace for recent immigrants since the Immigration Reform and Control Act of 1986

(IRCA) went into effect, and they are described in detail further on.

For the interview sample of fifty Central American immigrants, three social service agencies that catered primarily to Latin American immigrants were chosen as interview sites, and potential respondents were randomly selected from the case loads of the agencies. Two of the three agencies were privately run community-based agencies that received some funding from the D.C. government as well as from private sources. One of the agencies was heavily frequented by recent immigrants from Central American countries in search of referrals for employment, housing, food, and other basic needs. The second agency provided services for women with small children who had no other recourse for pre- and postnatal services. The third agency was a church-based organization that also provided employment, housing, educational, and other information on basic services available in the local community. This agency was authorized to provide English-language classes to immigrants who qualified for the general amnesty under the new immigration law. The three agencies were selected as sites for interviews because a majority of clients originated in the Central American countries, because they were among the best-known and most widely used agencies in the community, and because the directors of these agencies allowed me the use of their facilities for the interviews.

A snowball sampling method was also employed, as initial respondents were asked to suggest the names of relatives or friends who might be interested in participating in the study. This method was used at the onset of the research for the purpose of selecting and comparing roughly equal numbers of documented and undocumented Central Americans, as well as more recent immigrants and earlier arrivals. The difficulties of sampling recent Central American immigrants are evident, since a completely random survey of a largely undocumented population is impossible, as Cornelius (1982) cautioned. Aware of the potential pitfalls of drawing conclusions from a nonrandom snowball sample,[1] I used this information primarily to frame the questions for a survey that would gather data from a wider population of Central Americans as well as to enrich quantitative data with personal life histories. Most of the interviews were conducted on the premises of the social service agencies or in respondents' apartments or homes. When approached under the aegis of a social service agency or upon recommendations from friends or family members, very few of those who were asked to participate in the study refused to do so. Soliciting participants in this manner ensured that informants were more at ease in answering questions—a critical factor among largely undocumented immigrants who prefer to conceal their identities, since they are highly vulnerable and subject to deportation.

On the basis of information obtained in the interviews, certain neighborhoods and apartment buildings with large populations of Central American residents were targeted for a random survey.[2] This survey of one hundred randomly selected Central American households was conducted with the aid of four Salvadoran research assistants. Five different sites were selected in the District of Columbia and the Maryland and Virginia suburbs, and at each of the sites apartment buildings and housing complexes were identified as locations where many of the tenants originated in one of the Central American countries. Once buildings with a high proportion of Central American residents were selected, the research assistants made several attempts to contact tenants in targeted apartments before a substitute was chosen (in the case of absence or noncompliance). Interviewers used a standardized Spanish-language questionnaire form that collected detailed background and current information. This included age, sex, city of birth, education level, English-language proficiency, occupational histories of all household members, parental education and occupation, reasons for leaving the country of origin, reasons for choosing Washington as destination point, and personal aspirations. The survey also included questions about current and past employment in the Washington area, and about knowledge and perceptions of the new immigration law and its impact on individuals and families from Central American countries.

The analysis of data in the chapters was based primarily on this survey of one hundred households because it was a more random sample and because there were fewer possibilities for biases to cloud the information. The lengthier interviews issuing from the sample of fifty individuals, on the other hand, provided corroborating material as well as personal narratives and portraits of the people behind the statistics. These life histories particularly enriched the accounts of men's and women's role changes that have accompanied migration experiences. Finally, the interviews with seventy-five employers in the three major sectors where Central American migrants in Washington tend to be employed—in the construction, restaurant, and cleaning industries—provided more detailed information about employment conditions for Central American immigrants and about the impact of IRCA on area employers and workers.

In order to assess the impact of employer sanctions on the construction, restaurant, and domestic-services industries in the Washington area, field research was divided into three sections. I conducted interviews with employers in twenty-five large, medium, and small construction companies to gather information on the backgrounds of the companies, composition of the workforce, recruitment procedures for new workers, and the impact of IRCA on their businesses. Most of these were face-to-face interviews, but a few were done by telephone at the employer's request. Ten of the companies were owned and operated by permanent residents or citizens of Hispanic origin, and these were chosen at random from the *Guia Latina de Comercio 1989* for the Washington area. Fifteen construction companies, selected from the D.C. area yellow pages, the "Blue Book of Major Homebuilders" for the Washington area, and the *Washington Business Journal*'s annual list of the largest commercial developers in the Washington area, were owned by citizens born in the

United States. Businesses were selected so that the sample of small, medium, and large companies would be equally distributed among the District of Columbia, Maryland, and Northern Virginia.

I also conducted interviews with employers in two categories of restaurants. In the first category, employers of Hispanic origin in fifteen restaurants that served primarily Mexican or Central or South American cuisine were chosen from the *Guia Latina de Comercio 1989* for the Washington area. In the second category, twenty restaurants owned by U.S.-born citizens or people originating in non–Spanish speaking countries were chosen from the yellow pages after establishing a number of criteria for the selection (for example, no fast-food restaurants, bars, or drive-in restaurants were among those examined). Again, they were selected so that comparable numbers of small, medium, and large restaurants located in Washington, D.C., Maryland, and northern Virginia were represented.

Employers in ten companies that provided domestic, cleaning, or maintenance services were also interviewed. Five of the companies specialized in commercial and residential cleaning/maintenance and were chosen from the D.C. area yellow pages. The other five companies provided nannies, baby-sitters, and housekeepers for private employment, and these companies were selected because of their ongoing regular advertisements in the *Washington Post*. I also met with trade union officials in several construction trades to discuss questions about the national origin of union members, the union's position on the new immigration law, and the perceived impact of IRCA on the availability of construction jobs in the area.

Notes

Chapter One

1. As much as 20 percent of the population of El Salvador, or one million people, may have migrated to the United States in the 1980s, according to Montes Mozo and Vasquez (1988). Figures on the number of Central Americans in Washington vary greatly because of the large number of recent and undocumented immigrants among them. The *Washington Post* reported in 1987 that an estimated 80,000 Salvadorans lived in the District of Columbia and that up to 100,000 more resided in the surrounding suburbs (Pressley 1987). At its annual Festival of American Folklife in 1988, the Smithsonian Institution's scholars also estimated that approximately 200,000 Salvadorans resided in the metropolitan area. Preliminary 1990 census figures place the number of Hispanic-origin individuals in the Washington area at 230,000. But social service agency representatives say that many undocumented individuals remain uncounted because they were reluctant to respond to the census.

2. On the Central American migration to Los Angeles and other cities, see Donato 1992; Hamilton and Chinchilla 1991; Wallace 1986. On the migration to Washington, D.C., see Cohen 1980 and Repak 1990, 1994a.

3. See the Appendix for a more complete description of the methodology.

4. These are life histories of actual individuals, but their names have been changed to protect their privacy.

5. Only three countries in the world, the United States, Israel, and Argentina, attract more women than men as immigrants. See United

Nations 1979. It is estimated that about 10 million women have moved from rural to urban areas throughout Latin America since the mid-seventies. Approximately 8.5 million men have done the same. See Seager and Olson 1986; Orlansky and Dubrovsky 1978.

6. From Fernández-Kelly and Portes 1988. See also Portes 1978a; Portes and Bach 1985; Wood 1982.

7. Sassen-Koob 1986:1160.

8. Cornelius 1988; Fernández-Kelly 1983; Fernández-Kelly and Garcia 1988; Massey et al. 1987; Sassen-Koob 1986.

9. Donato 1992:166.

10. On Irish migration, see Diner 1983; on Jamaican migration, see Foner 1986.

11. See Bonacich 1976; Castells 1975; Piore 1979; Portes and Bach 1985.

12. See Anderson 1974; Lomnitz 1977; MacDonald and MacDonald 1974; Massey et al. 1987; Mines 1984; Tienda 1983; Tilly 1978.

13. Hondagneu 1990:9.

14. Borjas 1982; Chiswick 1978; Mincer 1970; Reimers 1985; Schulz 1961.

15. Borjas 1987; Cornelius 1988; Portes and Bach 1980; Tienda 1983.

16. Bonacich 1976; Edwards et al. 1975; Piore 1979; Portes and Bach 1985.

17. Concerning the New York Chinatown study, see Zhou and Logan 1989; on the larger study comparing Anglo and Hispanic-origin women, see Tienda and Guhleman 1985.

18. Bach 1985; Hamilton and Chinchilla 1991; Zolberg, Surke, and Aguayo 1986.

19. See Barker and Pianin 1988:A-21.

20. See Portes and Rumbaut 1990; Portes and Bach 1985.

21. Foner 1986.

22. See Grasmuck and Pessar 1991; Hondagneu-Sotelo 1992.

23. Fernández-Kelly 1983; Grasmuck and Pessar 1991; Hondagneu-Sotelo 1992; Pessar 1986.

Chapter Two

1. See Hamilton and Chinchilla 1991; Montes Mozo and Vasquez 1988; Ruggles and Fix 1985.

2. See Bach 1985; Bonacich and Cheng 1984; Hamilton and Chinchilla 1991; Portes 1983; Portes and Bach 1985.

3. See Hamilton and Chinchilla 1991; U.S. GAO 1989.

4. See Browning 1971; Bulmer-Thomas 1987; Hamilton and Chinchilla 1991; Woodward 1985.

5. A hectare is roughly equivalent to 2.47 acres. See Jung 1984.

6. The effect was so profound that Robert Williams described cotton production as a major force in the deterioration of the peasant family (Williams 1986:70). A plethora of works in recent decades has described the different and often adverse effects of capitalist development on women as opposed to men in third-world countries. See Hafkin and Bay 1976; Fernández-Kelly 1983; Orlansky and Dubrovsky 1978; Safa 1979.

7. Orlansky and Dubrovsky 1978:9.

8. Nieves 1979:139.

9. See Nieves 1979; Thomson 1986:34.

10. Between 1950 and 1961, 73 percent of all migrants moved to cities in El Salvador, 41 percent to San Salvador alone. See Hamilton and Chinchilla 1991; Nieves 1979; Orlansky and Dubrovsky 1978; Thomson 1986.

11. The expulsion orders ostensibly grew out of border disputes and trade rivalry between the two countries as Honduras became increasingly indebted to El Salvador. But the presence of 300,000 Salvadoran settlers in Honduran territory exacerbated tensions when economic troubles deepened, and Honduras expropriated the land of many of the peasants who had migrated from El Salvador.

12. As increasing numbers of landless peasants migrated to urban areas, only a small number of industrial jobs became available to the burgeoning urban workforce, since development strategies focused primarily on the capital-intensive export industry. Thomson 1986:23.

13. See Christian 1986:95.

14. Marti, who was executed after the insurrection, became one of the major inspirations for the armed insurrection of the 1980s, and the resistance movement eventually took his name—the Farabundo Marti National Liberation Front (Farabundo Martí de Liberación Nacional), or FMLN.

15. See Montgomery 1982.

16. Gettleman et al. 1986:51.

17. Montgomery 1982.

18. Christian 1986; Gettleman et al. 1986; Wilkinson 1993.

19. The American Sanctuary Movement was a loosely knit organization of churches and civil rights workers formed in 1982 to protect Central American refugees. It did so by arranging transport of refugees across Mexican and U.S. borders and by providing "safe houses" in the United States, places where undocumented refugees could stay until more-permanent housing could be found. It also aided in the processing and appeal of asylum applications in the United States.

20. In particular, several reports cited the massacre at the Sumpul River at the Honduran border and at El Mozote. Gettleman et al. 1986; U.S. Committee for Refugees 1984; Montes Mozo and Vasquez 1988; United Nations Truth Commission, cited in Wilkinson 1993.

21. The archbishop's assassins were later linked to former major Roberto D'Aubuisson, the young leader of a right-wing terrorist organization called the White Warriors Union. In April 1980 D'Aubuisson, who opposed the sweeping agrarian reform and the nationalization of banks proposed by the junta, led a right-wing coup that failed. He went on in the following year to form the National Republican Alliance (Alianza Republicana Nacional, or ARENA), which became the country's ruling conservative party.

22. Similarly high proportions of the Central Americans residing in the Washington area are highly educated and have white-collar professional backgrounds. For example, the women in the interview sample had completed an average of 10.7 years of school, and 27 percent had attended university at some point. Furthermore, 80 percent of respondents had resided in large cities in their countries of origin just before their migration to the United States; they were not peasants migrating directly from farms and villages. See Montes Mozo and Vasquez 1988; Repak 1990; Ruggles and Fix 1985; Wallace 1986.

23. Several Congressmen and Senators wrote critical reviews of the Reagan administration's reports, attempting to document the numerous instances in which it provided insufficient, misleading, and false information to Congress. One congressional report noted that "the Administration has at times appeared to take on the role of cheerleader rather than analyst in its military reports to Congress. . . . Under a more realistic evaluation, military aid is double that of our aid to reform and develop the economy. This reflects a military strategy devoted to prosecuting the civil war, and not one addressing the economic and social

problems leading to the civil war." The report stated that the administration supplied Congress with false information on the number of U.S. military personnel operating in El Salvador and on the roles they performed (U.S. Congress 1985). These charges were corroborated by a report in the *New York Times* (March 21, 1993) stating that "the Reagan Administration knew more than it publicly disclosed about some of the worst human rights abuses in El Salvador's civil war and withheld the information from Congress, declassified cables and interviews with former Government officials indicate."

24. See Painter 1987.

25. See Jung 1986; Thomson 1986.

26. As Table 3 demonstrates, 25 percent of respondents in the survey sample said that they left their countries of origin because of fighting in the area where they lived. When a further 14 percent, representing those who said they were forced to leave because of political persecution or death threats, is added to this first number, the figure climbs to 39 percent of survey respondents (48 percent of interviewees) who said that they fled their countries because of war, proximity to fighting, or personal danger and threats to family members. A majority of the respondents in this group originated in El Salvador.

27. Hamilton and Chinchilla 1991; Repak 1990; Stanley 1987.

28. See Krauss 1993; Wilkinson 1993.

29. Under the accords, the Salvadoran armed forces were cut in half, and a reviewing panel (approved by FMLN leaders) was to purge corrupt or brutal officers. Civil defense and paramilitary forces were ordered to disband, along with the military's intelligence directorate. A revamped civilian police force comprised primarily new recruits who could prove they had not been party to the earlier violence. A general amnesty and political freedoms for former rebels were also approved, so that moderate leftists could return from exile. Although the rebels gave up their claim to a share of power, they did wring key economic concessions from the conservative government. For example, the government agreed to secure some farmland in formerly rebel-held zones from wealthy families for the peasants living there. But in a visit to Chalatenango Province in El Salvador in early 1993, I was informed by U.N. development workers that none of the land in that province had been ceded as promised to the people working the land. The U.N. representatives said that the national government claimed it was unable to se-

cure the money necessary to reimburse the absentee landowners of large tracts in this and other provinces.

30. Painter 1987.

31. See Serafino 1989; Schultz 1989.

32. El Salvador's population of approximately 6 million comprises a smaller proportion of indigenous people (less than 10 percent) than does Guatemala or Nicaragua. With some six hundred people per square mile of arable land, El Salvador's high population density has had a profound effect on the movement of peoples within and out of the country. See Gettleman et al. 1986; Painter 1987.

33. Painter 1987.

34. Hamilton and Chinchilla 1991:106.

35. See Nieves 1979; Orlansky and Dubrovsky 1978.

36. These were the findings of the late Segundo Montes Mozo, one of the Jesuit priests from the Central American University in San Salvador who was murdered in 1989. He was a renowned sociologist who conducted a massive survey of Salvadoran families both in the United States and in El Salvador before his death. See Montes Mozo and Vasquez 1988.

Chapter Three

1. U.S. Census Office 1901 (as cited in Van Dyne 1984).

2. Pressley 1987.

3. Williams 1988.

4. A slow agricultural transformation in the South (with the enclosure movement and later mechanization) throughout the early 1900s led to the displacement of many African Americans, and they came in large numbers after both world wars—primarily fleeing political and economic oppression in the South. Migrants from the Carolinas generally made their way to Washington, Baltimore, Philadelphia, and New York. See Williams 1988.

5. Brinkley 1989.

6. Sassen-Koob 1986.

7. Lawrence 1988.

8. The Metropolitan Washington Council of Governments (COG) (1989b) projects population growth in the Washington area to be 32

percent between 1985 and 2010, while jobs in the same period are expected to grow by 65 percent (to reach 3.4 million). Employers experimented with various means to alleviate the labor shortage throughout the 1980s. Some attempted to attract workers from neighboring states, such as West Virginia and Pennsylvania, operating their own shuttle vans to bring in workers every morning. In an effort to recruit non-English-speaking employees, ten Arlington hotels offered classes in English and mathematics free of charge, in coordination with state and federal governments.

9. The counties included Falls Church, Fairfax, Arlington, and Alexandria in Virginia, and Montgomery in Maryland. Falls Church, Virginia, was the wealthiest, with $20,699 income per capita, which was double the national average of $10,797 for that year. See Rich 1988.

10. Power 1990:2.

11. Evans 1993:19 (quoting Washington, D.C., immigration lawyer Michael Maggio).

12. Women tend to compose the majority of the workforce in all domestic-service categories, whereas men form a significant presence only in commercial cleaning companies. Currently 50 percent of the workforce in many Washington-area cleaning companies is from El Salvador, and women who work part-time at night predominate.

13. No single group has predominated in the area's Hispanic business community, although Central and South Americans accounted for 44 percent of total business owners (four times the national average) in 1988. Conner 1988.

14. This figure is culled from local governments' health department statistics, which showed five thousand "food-service" entities operating throughout the metropolitan area in 1988. These food-service establishments included cafeterias, delicatessens, caterers, and hotels (with numerous kitchens, each counted separately).

15. Workers with documents could commute into the District, where, for example, hotels in 1988 paid $7 an hour for entry-level positions, as opposed to the $5-an-hour starting wage paid by hotels in northern Virginia. According to employment counselors, language skills were another factor in improving the bargaining position of workers; those who spoke some English could make more money in hospitals and in hotels than those who did not.

16. Pedraza (1992) and Portes and Bach (1985) define ethnic enclaves—such as the enclave created by Cuban exiles in Miami—as major centers for ethnically owned businesses that employ immigrants of similar ethnic origin.

17. One of the most visible signs of the greatly expanded Latin American community in Washington is the size of the Hispanic Heritage Festival, which is held annually in Adams Morgan in July. The festival attracted so many people to the neighborhood in 1988 (organizers estimated the crowd at around 300,000) that many local residents complained and agitated to have it moved. Thus, for the first time since its inception in 1970, the festival was held on the mall between the monuments in official downtown Washington in 1989. It is still considered to be the largest community festival in the city.

18. The study, based on a survey of 6,500 households, found that 82 percent of the poor population was black and 11 percent Hispanic. It concluded that Hispanics were the most seriously overrepresented racial or ethnic group among the poor, and that the figures were affected by the influx of poor immigrants from Latin American countries. Grier 1988.

19. Several social service agency representatives say that the difficulty of obtaining affordable housing in the area is more formidable than any other problem. Even if documented workers obtain jobs that pay above the minimum wage (at $5 or $6 per hour), they can hardly afford to live in most neighborhoods in and around Washington.

20. See Williams 1988.

21. The events in Washington preceded the Los Angeles riots in 1992 by almost a year, and the two disturbances have provoked commentaries concerning parallels between the situations in the two cities. Among the similarities, police-related actions triggered the rioting in Washington as well as in Los Angeles, and both events were fueled by perceptions of police brutality and widespread patterns of abuse. Latinos as well as African Americans rioted in Los Angeles, and half of those arrested afterward were Latinos. In both settings African Americans and Latin Americans have vied for power and influence in public offices, in the business community, and in civil rights mechanisms. In both cities African Americans appeared to compete more directly with Latin Americans than with any other group for jobs and scarce resources. Yet major differences between the two cities emerge. Most significantly, African Americans predominate on the police force in Washington, and

the numbers of newcomers from Latin American countries to the Washington area are much smaller than in Los Angeles County (which claimed 3.3 million Latinos by 1992). Equally important, immigrant workers in Washington do not appear to have displaced African Americans in inner-city jobs to the extent that they have in Los Angeles. Because the District of Columbia's Latin American community is of recent vintage and is not as entrenched as Los Angeles', D.C. Latinos have not yet attained political clout or mastered conventional means to secure assistance. On the L.A. riots, see Miles 1992.

22. D.C. Latino Civil Rights Task Force 1991.

23. Unemployment declined among African American youths in the District, from 31 percent in 1988 to 22 percent in 1989. See Metropolitan Washington Council of Governments 1989a; Grier 1988.

24. Bailey 1987; Cornelius 1988; Muller and Espenshade 1985.

Chapter Four

1. When using data or life histories from the initial sample of fifty in-depth interviews, I refer to the women or men *interviewed* in Washington. When using data from the larger, more random sample of one hundred Central American households, I refer to the men and women *surveyed* in Washington.

2. The term "recruitment" is used in a general sense here to indicate that a prospective migrant was asked by an employer (or an agent of that employer) to go to Washington for a specific job. Many employers in Washington also asked Central American women who were already working in that city to contact someone who would be willing to take a job in Washington. These types of arrangements can loosely be considered "informal labor recruitment," although it was sometimes difficult to determine whether it was the employers or friends/relatives already in Washington who initiated the work arrangements for prospective migrants.

3. See Van Dyne 1984:162.

4. Cohen 1980; Repak 1990, 1994a.

5. See also Romero 1992.

6. About half of the people interviewed knew the identity of the first member of their family to migrate to the Washington area and why that

original migrant chose to go to Washington. Close to half of the respondents whose relatives (the original migrants) were recruited to work in Washington were women who took jobs as domestics or child-care providers, and in 43 percent of these cases the female relative went to work for a diplomatic family. Among the 36 percent who were male relatives recruited to work in Washington, the majority took construction jobs that had been arranged by friends.

7. Cornelius 1988; Romero 1992.

8. On Mexican migration patterns, see Cornelius 1988; Hondagneu-Sotelo 1992; Portes and Bach 1985. On Dominican migration, see Grasmuck and Pessar 1991.

9. Foner 1986; Grasmuck and Pessar 1991; Hondagneu-Sotelo 1992.

10. On Italian immigration, see Kessner 1977; on Irish immigration, see Diner 1983.

11. See Glenn 1988; Katzman 1978; Romero 1988.

12. Glenn 1988; Romero 1988, 1992.

Chapter Five

1. Chiswick 1978; Mincer 1970; Schultz 1961.

2. Cornelius 1988; Portes and Bach 1980; Tienda 1983; Tienda et al. 1984; Zhou and Logan 1989.

3. Washington was never known as a strong union town, even though close to 80 percent of the construction work in the 1970s was handled by union contractors. By the end of the 1980s barely 10 to 15 percent of construction projects were under union contracts. Trade union officials interviewed in Washington gave several reasons for the sharp drop in membership and in the number of contracts won by union shops. First, the influx of Latin American workers in the 1980s, many of whom did not speak English, made organizing more difficult than it had been in the past. Second, many out-of-town contractors moved into the regional construction scene in the 1980s, bringing their own workers with them. Third, the Association of Building Contractors made a concerted effort to promote nonunion work, and they have spent millions of dollars since 1982 to lure nonunion contractors to the Washington area.

4. Analysis in this section is drawn primarily from the survey sample of one hundred Central American households. Only one man in this survey sample was unemployed at the time of the interviews, yielding an extremely low unemployment rate that was close to the average in 1988–89 for several of the counties in Virginia and Maryland surrounding the District of Columbia.

5. Beneria and Roldan 1987; Bunster and Chaney 1985; Chinchilla 1977; Jelin 1977; Nash and Safa 1976; Orlansky and Dubrovsky 1978.

6. Glenn 1988; Rollins 1985; Romero 1992.

7. Glenn 1988:143.

8. See also Rollins 1985.

9. Glenn 1988.

10. Despite their many human capital advantages over Mexicans, Central American men in California did not show higher income levels, unlike their Central American counterparts in Washington, who did enjoy significantly higher wages than other Latin American immigrants in the United States. Wallace (1986) suggested that the inability of Central American men to capitalize on their background characteristics may mean that they are being incorporated into California's economy in the same way as Mexican immigrants (e.g., in secondary-sector jobs). In other words, if Central Americans enter the same stratified labor market as Mexican immigrants, personal characteristics do not lead to higher incomes. On the other hand, Central American women have advantages over Mexican immigrant women in English-language proficiency, education level, and occupational background, and they appear to translate these variables into higher earnings.

11. In this chapter, structural variables refer to characteristics of the labor market and of the firms that employ immigrants. I also consider social networks in a structural context, although recent writings (Coleman, 1990, 1988) pinpoint networks as sources of social capital. I use a conventional definition of human capital variables, with an emphasis on education, English-language proficiency, length of time in the United States, and legal status.

12. For the purpose of analyzing the wage and employment data with multivariate linear regressions, only the data from the sample of one hundred Central American households are employed here. The lengthier interviews with informants in the smaller sample provided corroborating evidence for some of the findings, and they enriched the data

by providing personal histories as well. Also, variations between this smaller sample and the larger sample provided a context for making interesting comparisons in the following human capital variables: education level, English-speaking ability, length of time in the United States, and legal status.

13. On Los Angeles wage rates, see Cornelius 1988; on San Diego, see Chavez 1992; on San Francisco, see Menjivar 1993; on Houston, see Rodriguez 1987. The overall national average wage for service jobs in 1991 was $8.30, while construction workers nationally averaged $13.34 (according to the Bureau of Labor Statistics). The wide disparity in wage levels for different cities and immigrant groups is primarily attributable to structural factors: that is, the types of occupations open to men in Washington (particularly in the construction industry), the health of the local economy, the persistent labor shortage, and the concentration of immigrant men in primary-sector companies. Other structural influences on wage levels may include the minimum wage, unionism, and access to unemployment insurance.

14. Men who earned less than the median of $320 a week were classified as low earners; those who earned over $320 a week were classified as high earners. Men were categorized under the low/no-mobility heading if they averaged less than a $25 increase in salary per annum. Those whose wages increased by at least $35 per annum were classified under the high-mobility heading. None of the male respondents fell in between; none had a $25 to $35 increase in wages per annum.

15. Whether legal status has much bearing on wage levels is a heavily contested issue. One early pre-IRCA study showed that wage rates of undocumented migrants were influenced in the same way as those for legal immigrants—by level of education, labor market experience, and length of time in the United States—and thus that legal status did not affect wages. Other studies found the opposite: that undocumented workers earned significantly less than documented workers. One researcher explained that undocumented migrants earn lower wages than documented migrants because of their generally lower levels of human capital and their inadequate social networks. Others echoed these findings, that differences in wages are probably due to limitations in social networks rather than to lack of documentation. If undocumented workers make good use of social networks and have access to information

about the local labor market, then legal status will have little effect on wages. See Massey 1987; Morales 1983; Simon and DeLey 1986.

16. When the wage variable and human capital variables were categorized at the median for each sex, education had no significant association with higher wages for men in the survey sample ($\chi^2 > .05$). While length of time in the United States, legal status, and proficiency in English showed some effect on wages for men, these associations may have been confounded by the strong association between construction work and high wages. In order to control for possible confounding and to assess the independent predictors for wages, I used a multivariate linear regression model with weekly wages as a continuous variable (although, because of the small sample size, the study could not conclusively demonstrate significant differences). Social capital variables (Coleman 1988), such as having their first jobs arranged for them or finding their current jobs through social networks, were weakly significant for men, as were human capital variables, such as level of education and proficiency in English. Undocumented status had no measurable impact on wage levels.

17. Hondagneu-Sotelo 1992; Salzinger 1991.

18. Mean wages were calculated on the basis of a forty-hour work week, even though the work hours of domestics and child-care providers may vary widely. Live-in housekeepers, for example, are often asked to work evenings and weekends and may put in anywhere between sixty and ninety hours a week on the job. Women with daily housecleaning jobs, on the other hand, may work about five or six hours each day if they clean only one house per day.

19. Women who earned less than the median of $210 a week were classified as low earners, while those who earned $210 or more a week were classified as high earners. Women were also categorized under the low/no-mobility heading if they averaged less than a $25 increase in salary per annum. Those whose wages increased by at least $25 per annum were classified under the high-mobility heading. When the wage variable and human capital variables were categorized for these two groups, none of the variables were associated with higher wages ($\chi^2 > .05$).

20. This is the case for women in the survey sample, the majority of whom arrived in the United States in the 1980s (primarily after the

amnesty deadline), but not necessarily for the women in the interview sample, who had been in the country longer on average.

21. It must be borne in mind that the interview sample was not random; clients as well as several staff members who had once been clients of the social service agencies were among the respondents. Therefore a number of counselors and secretaries were preselected for this sample. None of the women in the survey sample had moved out of low-status and low-paying jobs as domestics or restaurant personnel into positions as teachers or counselors in social service agencies, as some of their counterparts in the interview sample had. Several from the survey sample had moved into jobs in offices, stores, or banks; one had become a seamstress and one a beautician. Only one woman, the highest-paid woman in the sample, had moved into a secretarial position after three years in the United States.

22. Fernández-Kelly and Garcia 1988; Sassen-Koob 1986; Simon and DeLey 1986.

23. Glenn 1988; Katzman 1978; Romero 1992.

24. Tienda et al. 1984, discussed in Grasmuck and Pessar 1991:187.

25. Verdugo 1982:9, discussed in Grasmuck and Pessar 1991:188.

26. Portes and Rumbaut 1990.

27. Wallace 1986.

28. Portes and Rumbaut 1990.

29. Women bring over relatives and sponsor other family members more readily than do men, perhaps because women are willing to assist sisters, cousins, and friends who support children and family members or who head households back home.

30. On Dominicans in New York, see Grasmuck and Pessar 1991; on Mexicans, see Fernández-Kelly and Garcia 1988; Simon and De Ley 1986.

31. Studies focusing on immigrant women's economic experiences have not been extensive, and this is particularly true of Central American women. Since the research has indicated that economic performance varies widely among groups of different national origin, it is important not to generalize to all Hispanic-origin women. Furthermore, it must be borne in mind that a large number of respondents in my samples were undocumented, whereas many earlier studies focused on legal immigrants.

Chapter Six

1. The directors of two social service agencies said in the interviews that the majority of the people who call their agencies looking for domestic help do not ask specifically for documented workers, and some even express an interest in helping women who are undocumented.

2. The law established a ceiling of 290,000 immigrants to be allowed entry each year, 20,000 from any given country. These numbers were virtually meaningless because immediate family members of U.S. citizens were subject to no limits but were nonetheless counted against the ceiling figures, and because no laws curtailed the even greater number of undocumented immigrants entering the country every year. The limitations were contained under a set of six "preferences," or categories. Four of the categories were reserved for various types of relatives, and the remaining two (which comprised 10 percent of available visas) were reserved for people with desirable occupational skills. Later, the Refugee Act of 1980 eliminated refugees as a category of the preference system and set 270,000 as the worldwide ceiling for immigrants, exclusive of refugees.

3. Identity and employment eligibility may be established by a U.S. passport, a certificate of citizenship or naturalization, a foreign passport with employment authorization, or an alien registration card, or by a combination of a state-issued drivers license or U.S. military card with an original social security card, a U.S. birth certificate, or an unexpired INS employment authorization card.

4. The penalties levied against employers who employ undocumented migrants range between $250 and $2,000 per unauthorized employee for a first violation and up to $10,000 for subsequent violations (after the second). Employers who fail to comply with the record-keeping requirements (retaining in their files an I-9 form for every employee) face civil fines between $100 and $1,000 for each employee with improperly completed forms. Under the new law, employers can also be penalized for engaging in discriminatory practices (e.g., refusing to hire persons with "foreign-sounding names" or with foreign accents) or for requiring from an individual a bond or indemnity against liability (e.g., making an undocumented employee pay "insurance" against the risk of the employer's being fined for hiring him or her). U.S. Immigration and Naturalization Service 1986.

5. The amnesty provision failed to clarify the status of family members who were ineligible for amnesty in their own right, and therefore it raised fears that families would be separated if some family members (especially minors) were deported while others received amnesty. Employers and private-interest groups maintained that the employer-sanctions section created problems for U.S. citizens because many Americans could not produce social security cards or birth certificates to prove their nativity. Employers complained that it was unreasonable to require documents from such employees, since it was a long and cumbersome process for some people born in distant states to track down birth certificates and appropriate documents.

6. The U.S. Department of Labor has promulgated a complicated set of procedures whereby employers must post ads in the local press for a certain period of time for each position and must fill out lengthy forms for the employee. The petition must be forwarded to the Department of Labor, which certifies that the occupation is in short supply of workers. After the employer shows that he or she is unable to find a U.S. citizen or an authorized alien to fill a particular position, a prospective employee can receive work authorization. The process used to take from one to three years, but now finalization may take as long as ten years. Employment-based certification is one of the main avenues open to women who seek employment in domestic service.

7. Refugees may apply for political asylum through a lawyer or a social service agency, and they must be able to prove that persecution is a reasonable possibility if they were to return to the country of origin.

8. A California judge eventually barred the Reagan administration from deporting Salvadorans in violation of their rights under the Refugee Act of 1980. He noted that the methods the INS was using to coerce and intimidate Salvadorans into abandoning their asylum claims and "voluntarily" going home ranged "from subtle persuasion to outright threats and misrepresentations." He said that this was "not the result of isolated transgressions from a few overzealous officers," but rather resulted "from INS policies, and form[ed] a pattern and practice of illegal conduct which [was] approved, authorized, and/or ratified by INS personnel at all levels." See Frelick 1988.

9. The bill was one outcome of the American Baptist Church case, a massive 1985 lawsuit filed by more than eighty religious and refugee organizations (including the American Sanctuary Movement). The bill

halted all deportations of Salvadorans and Guatemalans and required the INS to give them work permits until new asylum applications were reviewed. It was expected to affect 15,000 to 20,000 Central Americans in the Washington area, and up to 500,000 nationwide. As of April 1991 the Washington, D.C., area had one of the largest TPS registrant populations in the country.

10. A detailed discussion of the methodology employed in the employer interviews can be found in the Appendix.

11. In total, a relatively small number of firms were cited or fined in Maryland, Northern Virginia, and Washington largely because of a lack of officers to enforce the employer sanctions provisions (e.g., there were only five enforcement officers for all of Maryland in 1989). The Maryland branch of the INS claimed that by 1990, fourteen employers in Maryland construction firms and twelve in the service industry had received fines since IRCA went into effect, and 194 "aliens" had been apprehended (they were evenly divided between construction companies and services, and the majority were of Salvadoran origin). In Washington, D.C., and northern Virginia, only two employers in construction companies and eleven in the service industry had received fines.

12. Similarly, employers in the cleaning industry were defensive about the "fact" that foreign-born workers did not take jobs away from Americans, since African Americans were not interested in commuting to distant suburbs to work. These employers maintained that a majority of employees who cleaned buildings in the suburbs were of Latin American origin, while employees who worked in District of Columbia buildings were predominantly African Americans.

13. See note 3 to Chapter 5.

14. In the long run, one heavier cost may be that employers can discriminate against workers who are obviously foreign-born (e.g., those with accents or who "look different"), and they can get rid of such employees under various pretexts. Several U.S. government agencies are studying such issues as the incidence of discrimination in hiring practices after the passage of IRCA and the impact of employer sanctions on U.S.- and foreign-born workers.

15. U.S. Department of Labor 1991:126.

16. Part of the reason for this may be that wages in the Washington area were already significantly higher than wages for comparable jobs in other large cities in the United States, as Chapter Five shows.

17. Wayne Cornelius of the University of California's Center for U.S.-Mexican Studies, quoted in Suro 1989.

18. U.S. Department of Labor 1991:50. This report was mandated by Congress to assess the efficacy of IRCA's employer sanctions in achieving its intended goal of protecting jobs for qualified U.S. workers. As a contributor to the study, I analyzed the extent of IRCA's impact on Washington-area businesses and workers; to that end I interviewed numerous employers in the construction, restaurant, and cleaning industries (where Central American workers are concentrated).

19. Some noted that most European countries allow in temporary workers for employment in specific industries—a more organized means of controlling immigration and of helping to alleviate labor shortages in certain industries. Three restaurant employers suggested that just as agricultural conglomerates and other farm employers are able to obtain temporary workers on contract, so restaurants and other ailing industries should be allowed access to temporary workers. One employer noted that restaurants, as the fifth most powerful industry in the United States, should have the same access to temporary workers that growers and farmers do.

20. U.S. Department of Labor 1991:127.

21. U.S. Department of Labor 1991:124. The economic effects of immigration are complex and have spawned a vitriolic debate about whether immigrant workers form a substitute or complement to the U.S. workforce. Recent studies have demonstrated that variations in the characteristics of regional labor markets and in sectors of the economy determine how differently immigrant workers are received (Cornelius 1988; Bailey 1987; Muller and Espenshade 1985). Some industries, regions, groups, and employees may benefit from an influx of immigrant workers, while others may suffer. Variations depend largely upon the location within the United States, on the state of the local economy, and on the sector of employment or industry concerned. Growers in the western states, for example, had few problems finding enough people to pick fruit and vegetables in 1988, and California's restaurants and janitorial service companies did not report major labor shortages. But certain industries have been quick to blame the new law for their labor problems. According to the 1980 census, more than 25 percent of undocumented migrants in the United States work in manufacturing (half

of them in apparel and textile factories), predominantly in New York and southern California. Garment manufacturers in the Los Angeles area, particularly those that employ Hispanics, reported severe labor shortages at the end of 1988 and blamed the situation on the new immigration law. Owners of large factories complained that their businesses were threatened by small contractors who continued to hire undocumented workers in Los Angeles factories and sweatshops.

Chapter Seven

1. Grasmuck and Pessar 1991; Hondagneu-Sotelo 1992; Pessar 1986.

2. Grasmuck and Pessar 1991; Pedraza 1991.

3. The lengthy open-ended interviews with women in the sample of fifty Central American individuals were particularly useful in exploring the impact of the migration experience on gender roles and on women's lives and relationships. Thirty women offered detailed responses to questions about their responsibilities in the home, their relationships with partners and family members, how the migration experience had altered these relationships, and what they aspired to be in their adopted country. This chapter's discussion on gender roles and the migration experience is based primarily on the interview sample. The women in the interview sample were representative of the survey sample in that comparable proportions were married or living with a companion and had children living with them (over half the samples) and most women worked full-time outside the home. Like their counterparts in the survey sample, a majority of the women entered the wage-labor force in the United States in domestic service and over half were still working in that capacity at the time of the interviews. For this reason I am confident that many of the women's perceptions about changes in gender roles accurately reflect the perceptions of Central American women in Washington generally.

4. Consuela claims that the sex ratio in Washington is a major element contributing to women's elevated status in the United States. She believes that in Washington there are more single Central American men from her native region than there are single women, which makes it

more difficult for men to meet and maintain relationships with other women outside of their established households.

5. Fernández-Kelly and Garcia 1988; Kibria 1990; Pessar 1984, 1986.

6. Grasmuck and Pessar 1991.

7. Fernández-Kelly and Garcia 1988:2.

8. Grasmuck and Pessar 1991.

9. Only one woman among the thirty interviewed in Washington was prevented from working outside the home by a husband who felt that she should remain at home with their children.

10. In response, local governments and private sources have established programs within the social service agencies and churches to deal specifically with substance abuse and other youth-related problems, instituting widely used drug-counseling and education programs for both children and their parents.

11. Several women noted that at the very least they were safe from political persecution and that their children would not be drafted into the army. As Carmen exclaimed, "Here we don't have to be afraid of fighting or that someone will kill us or take us away in the night."

12. A further 10 percent planned to reside permanently in the United States but wished to relocate to California; 6 percent wanted to live in Mexico or in Europe someday.

13. Chavez 1992:184.

Chapter Eight

1. Rodriguez (1987) wrote about the ways in which Central American immigrants in Houston formed new migration patterns in that city.

2. Rodriguez 1987:9.

3. On California figures, see Cornelius 1988; on Houston, see Rodriguez 1987.

4. Tienda and Guhleman 1985; Zhou and Logan 1989.

5. See Pedraza 1991:321.

6. In 1993 follow-up interviews with the women in the interview sample, twenty of the twenty-two women I was able to contact had attained legal status—or 90 percent of the respondents who were reinterviewed.

Appendix

1. As Grasmuck and Pessar (1991:58) note, a snowball sample is a nonprobability sampling procedure in which cases are initially deliberately selected on the basis of particular variables and then expanded by means of referrals or contacts from the early interviews: "The snowball sample, being unrepresentative, involves the risk of unrecognized biases in regard to other variables. It is possible, however, to evaluate the overall representativeness of a snowball sample by comparing it on key variables with other representative samples of the subject population."

2. In this type of cross-cultural research, a truly random sample is only possible when the population is homogeneous and an accurate and current roster of names and addresses can be used as a sampling base. Neither of these factors was applicable in the case of Central American immigrants because the population was not homogeneous (immigrants varied by country, education level, class background, and other factors); most immigrants arrived after the 1980 census and refused to cooperate with the 1990 census; and they made every attempt to remain uncounted and off official rosters or address lists (the majority were undocumented). As Cornelius (1982:5) explained, "A clandestine population cannot be sampled through any strict randomization procedure, and the total number of cases which can be observed or interviewed is likely to be substantially smaller than in the conventional sample survey, regardless of the sampling procedure."

Bibliography

Anderson, Grace M. 1974. *Networks of Contact: The Portuguese and Toronto.* Waterloo, Ont.: Wilfrid Laurier University Press.

Applebome, P. 1988. "Amnesty Requests by Aliens Decline." *New York Times,* January 3.

Arizpe, Lourdes. 1977. "Women in the Informal Labor Sector: The Case of Mexico City." *Signs* 3, no.1:25–37.

Arocha, Zita. 1988. "Salvadoran Draft Register Ruled Eligible for Asylum." *Washington Post,* October 14.

Bach, Robert. 1985. *Western Hemispheric Immigration to the U.S.: A Review of Selected Research Trends.* Washington, D.C.: Center for Immigration Policy and Refugee Assistance, Georgetown University.

Bailey, Thomas. 1987. *Immigrant and Native Workers: Contrasts and Competition.* Boulder, Colo.: Westview.

Barker, Kathleen, and Edith Pianin. 1988. "The Wait for Reprieve or Return." *Washington Post,* March 4.

Bean, Frank, Gray Swicegood, and Allan King. 1985. "Role Incompatibility and the Relationship Between Fertility and Labor Supply Among Hispanic Women." In *Hispanics in the U.S. Economy,* ed. George Borjas and Marta Tienda. New York: Academic Press.

Beneria, Lourdes, and Martha Roldan. 1987. *The Crossroads of Class and Gender.* Chicago: University of Chicago Press.

Bonacich, Edna. 1976. "Advanced Capitalism and Black/White Relations: A Split Labor Market Interpretation." *American Sociological Review* 41:34–51.

Bonacich, Edna, and Lucie Cheng. 1984. "Introduction: A Theoretical Orientation to International Labor Migration." In *Labor Immigra-*

tion Under Capitalism: Asian Workers in the United States Before World War Two, ed. Edna Bonacich et al. Berkeley and Los Angeles: University of California Press.

Borjas, George. 1990. "Self-Selection and the Earnings of Immigrants: Reply." *American Economic Review* 80, no.1:3058.

———. 1987. "Self-Selection and the Earnings of Immigrants." *American Economic Review* 77, no.4:531–53.

———. 1985. "Assimilation, Changes in Cohort Quality, and the Earnings of Immigrants." *Journal of Labor Economics* 3, no.4:463–89.

———. 1982. "The Earnings of Male Hispanic Immigrants in the United States." *Industrial and Labor Relations Review* 5, no.3: 343–53.

Borjas, George, and Marta Tienda, eds. 1985. *Hispanics in the U.S. Economy.* New York: Academic Press.

Boserup, Esther. 1970. *Woman's Role in Economic Development.* New York: St. Martin's Press.

Brinkley, David. 1989. *Washington Goes to War.* New York: Penguin.

Browning, David. 1971. *El Salvador: Landscape and Society.* Oxford: Clarendon Press.

Bulmer-Thomas, Victor. 1987. *The Political Economy of Central America Since 1920.* Cambridge: Cambridge University Press.

Bunster, Ximena, and Elsa Chaney. 1985. *Sellers and Servants: Working Women in Lima, Peru.* New York: Praeger.

Cadaval, Olivia. 1988. "Adams Morgan: New Identity for an Old Neighborhood." In *Washington at Home: Neighborhoods in the Nation's Capital,* ed. Kathleen Schneider Smith. Washington, D.C.: Windsor Publications.

Castells, Manuel. 1975. "Immigrant Workers and Class Struggles in Advanced Capitalism: The Western European Experience," *Politics and Society* 5:1.

Chaney, Elsa, and Marianne Schmink. 1976. "Women and Modernization: Access to Tools." In *Sex and Class in Latin America,* ed. June Nash and Helen Safa. New York: Praeger.

Chavez, Leo. 1992. *Shadowed Lives: Undocumented Immigrants in American Society.* Philadelphia: Harcourt Brace Jovanovich.

Chinchilla, Norma. 1977. "Industrialization, Monopoly Capital, and Women's Work in Guatemala." *Signs* 3, no.1:38–56.

Chiswick, Barry. 1984. "Illegal Aliens in the United States Labor Market: Analysis of Occupational Attainment and Earnings." *International Migration Review* 18, no.3:714–32.

———. 1980. "Immigrant Earnings Patterns by Sex, Race, and Ethnic Groupings." *Monthly Labor Review,* October, 22–25.

———. 1978. "The Effect of Americanization on the Earnings of Foreign-Born Men." *Journal of Political Economy* 86, no.5:897–921.

Christian, Shirley. 1986. "El Salvador's Divided Military." In *El Salvador: Central America in the New Cold War,* ed. Marvin Gettleman et al. New York: Grove Press.

Cobb Clark, Deborah. 1990. "Migrant and Immigration Policy Selectivity: The Impact on the Wages of Married Foreign-Born Women." Paper prepared for the U.S. Department of Labor, Division of Immigration Policy and Research.

Cohen, Lucy. 1980. "Stress and Coping Among Latin American Women Immigrants." In *Uprooting and Development: Dilemmas of Coping with Modernization,* ed. George V. Coelho and Paul I. Ahmed. New York: Plenum Press.

Coleman, James S. 1990. *Foundations of Social Theory.* Cambridge, Mass: Belknap Press.

———. 1988. "Social Capital in the Creation of Human Capital." *American Journal of Sociology* 94:S95–S120.

Conner, P. 1988. *Hispanic Business Enterprise Focus: Greater Washington, D.C. Business Sector.* Kansas City: U.S. Hispanic Chamber of Commerce.

Cornelius, Wayne. 1988. "Los Migrantes de la Crisis: The Changing Profile of Mexican Labor Migration to California in the 1980s." Paper presented at the conference "Population and Work in Regional Settings," El Colegio de Michoacan, Zamora, Michoacan, November 28–30.

———. 1982. *Interviewing Undocumented Immigrants: Methodological Reflections Based on Fieldwork in Mexico and the United States.* San Diego, Calif.: U.C.S.D. Program for U.S.-Mexican Studies.

Cue, Reynaldo, and Robert Bach. 1980. "The Return of the Clandestine Worker and the End of the Golden Exile." In *Sourcebook on the New Immigration,* ed. Roy S. Bryce-Laporte. New Jersey: Transaction Books.

Davis, P. 1988. "New Migrants Fill Tent Cities." *Washington Post,* July 10.

D.C. Latino Civil Rights Task Force. 1991. *The Latino Blueprint for Action.* Washington, D.C.: Latino Civil Rights Task Force.

Diner, Hasia. 1983. *Erin's Daughters in America.* Baltimore: Johns Hopkins University Press.

Dinnerman, Ina. 1978. "Patterns of Adaptation Among Households of U.S.-Bound Migrants from Michoacan, Mexico." *International Migration Review* 12, no.4:485–501.

Donato, Katharine. 1992. "Understanding U.S. Immigration: Why Some Countries Send Women and Others Send Men." In *Seeking Common Ground: Multidisciplinary Studies of Immigrant Women in the U.S.,* ed. Donna Gabaccia. Westport, Conn.: Praeger.

Durham, William. 1979. *Scarcity and Survival in Central America.* Stanford, Calif.: Stanford University Press.

Edwards, R. C. et al. 1975. *Labor Market Segmentation.* Lexington, Mass.: D. C. Heath.

Evans, Sandra. 1993. "In Affluent Homes, the Nanny Dilemma Isn't News." *Washington Post,* February 7, A-1.

Fernández-Kelly, Maria Patricia. 1989. "Power Surrendered, Power Restored." In *Women, Change and Politics,* ed. Louise Tilley and Patricia Guerin. New York: Russell Sage.

―――. 1983. *For We Are Sold, I and My People: Women and Industry in Mexico's Frontier.* Albany: State University of New York Press.

Fernández-Kelly, Maria Patricia, and Anna Garcia. 1988. "Invisible Amidst the Glitter: Hispanic Women in the Southern California Electronics Industry." In *The Worth of Women's Work,* ed. Anne Statham et al. Albany: State University of New York Press.

Fernández-Kelly, Maria Patricia, and Alejandro Portes. 1988. "A Continent on the Move: Immigrants and Refugees in the Americas." Unpublished paper prepared for the Other Americas Project, WGBH Educational Foundation.

Foner, Nancy. 1986. "Sex Roles and Sensibilities: Jamaican Women in New York and London." In *International Migration: The Female Experience,* ed. Rita Simon and Carolyn Brettell. Totowa, N.J.: Rowman & Allanheld.

Forella, P. 1989. "The Changing Face of Labor." *Washington Business Journal Magazine,* May.

Frelick, Bill. 1988. "The Mistreated Refugees from El Salvador." *Washington Post,* May 3.

Gettleman, Marvin, Patrick Lacefield, Louis Menashe, and David Mermelstein, eds. 1986. *El Salvador: Central America in the New Cold War.* New York: Grove Press.

Gill, Andrew, and Stewart Long. 1989. "Is There an Immigration Status Wage Differential Between Legal and Undocumented Workers? Evidence from the Los Angeles Garment Industry." *Social Science Quarterly* 70, no.1:164–73.

Gleijeses, Piero. 1984. "Perspectives of a Regime Transformation in Guatemala." In *Political Change in Central America,* ed. Wolf Grabendorff et al. Boulder, Colo.: Westview.

Glenn, Evelyn Nakano. 1988. "A Belated Industry Revised: Domestic Service Among Japanese-American Women." In *The Worth of Women's Work,* ed. Anne Statham et al. Albany: State University of New York Press.

Grabendorf, Wolf, et al., eds. 1984. *Political Change in Central America.* Boulder, Colo.: Westview.

Grasmuck, Sherri, and Patricia Pessar. 1991. *Between Two Islands: Dominican International Migration.* Berkeley and Los Angeles: University of California Press.

Grier, George. 1988. *Special Report: Greater Washington's Labor Shortage.* Washington, D.C.: Greater Washington Research Center.

Grier, George, and Eunice Grier. 1985. *Greater Washington at Mid-Decade.* Washington, D.C.: Greater Washington Research Center.

Hafkin, Nancy, and Edna Bay. 1976. *Women in Africa.* Stanford, Calif.: Stanford University Press.

Hamilton, Nora, and Norma Chinchilla. 1991. "Central American Migration: A Framework for Analysis." *Latin American Research Review* 26, no.1:75–110.

Harrington, Walter. 1988. "Prisoners of Overachievement." *Washington Post Magazine,* November 13.

Heer, D. M., and D. Falasco. 1983. "Determinants of Earnings Among Three Groups of Mexican Americans: Undocumented Immigrants, Legal Immigrants, and the Native Born." Paper presented at the annual meetings of the Population Association of America, Minneapolis.

Hilzenrath, D. 1989. "Washington Area Leads in Office Construction." *Washington Post,* February 11.

Holden, C. 1988. "Debate Warming Up on Legal Migration Policy." *Science* 241:288.

Hondagneu, Pierette. 1990. *Gender and the Politics of Mexican Undocumented Immigrant Settlement.* PhD. diss., University of California at Berkeley.

Hondagneu-Sotelo, Pierette. 1992. "Overcoming Patriarchal Constraints: The Reconstruction of Gender Relations Among Mexican Immigrant Men and Women." *Gender and Society* 6, no.3:393–415.

Jasso, Guillermina, and Mark Rosenzweig. 1990. "Self-Selection and the Earnings of Immigrants: Comment." *American Economic Review* 80, no.1:298–304.

Jelin, Elizabeth. 1977. "Migration and Labor Force Participation of Latin American Women: The Domestic Servants in the Cities." *Signs* 3, no.1:133.

Jordan, M. 1987. "Many Roads Blocked for Salvadorans." *Washington Post,* July 30.

Jung, Harald. 1986. "Class Struggle and Civil War in El Salvador." In *El Salvador: Central America in the New Cold War,* ed. Marvin Gettleman et al. New York: Grove Press.

———. 1984. "The Civil War in El Salvador." In *Political Change in Central America,* ed. Wolf Grabendorff and Heinrich Krumwiede. Boulder, Colo.: Westview.

Katzman, David. 1978. *Seven Days a Week: Women and Domestic Service in Industrial America.* New York: Oxford University Press.

Kessner, Thomas. 1977. *The Golden Door: Italian and Jewish Immigrant Mobility in New York City, 1880–1915.* New York: Oxford University Press.

Kibria, Nazli. 1990. "Power, Patriarchy, and Gender Conflict." *Gender and Society* 4:924.

Knight, Athelia. 1988. "D.C. on Way to Full Employment." *Washington Post,* July 30.

Kossoudji, S. A., and S. I. Ranney. 1984. "Wage Rates of Temporary Mexican Migrants to the U.S.: The Role of Legal Status." Paper presented at the Econometric Society Meeting, Dallas.

Kotkin, J. 1989. "The Future is Here." *Washington Post Magazine,* June 25.

Krauss, Clifford. 1993. "How U.S. Actions Helped Hide Salvador Human Rights Abuses." *New York Times,* March 21, A-1.

Lawrence, B. 1988. "New Index Ranks Area Economy Fourth Healthiest." *Washington Post,* October 31.

Lee, E. S. 1966. "A Theory of Migration." *Demography* 3:47–57.

Lewis, Roger K. 1987. *Shaping the City.* Washington, D.C.: AIA Press.

Lomnitz, Larissa. 1977. *Networks and Marginality: Life in a Mexican Shantytown.* New York: Academic Press.

Long, James. 1980. "The Effect of Americanization on Earnings: Some Evidence for Women." *Journal of Political Economy* 88, no.3:620–29.

MacDonald, John, and Leatrice MacDonald. 1974. "Chain Migration, Ethnic Neighborhood Formation, and Social Networks." In *An Urban World,* ed. Charles Tilley. Boston: Little, Brown.

Martin, Linda, and Kerry Segrave. 1985. *The Servant Problem: Domestic Workers in North America.* Jefferson, N.C.: McFarland.

Massey, Douglas S. 1987. "Do Undocumented Migrants Earn Lower Wages Than Legal Immigrants? New Evidence from Mexico." *International Migration Review* 21, no.2:236–74.

Massey, Douglas, Rafael Alarcón, Jorge Durand, and Humbert Gonzalez. 1987. *Return to Aztlán: The Social Process of International Migration from Western Mexico.* Berkeley and Los Angeles: University of California Press.

Masters, B. 1989. " '87 Law Cut Illegal Immigration, Study Says." *Washington Post,* July 14.

Menjivar, Cecilia. 1993. "Salvadorean Migration to the U.S. in the 1980s: What Can We Learn from It?" Paper presented at SECOLAS Conference, Antigua, Guatemala, February 19.

Metropolitan Washington Council of Governments. 1989a. *Economic Trends in Metropolitan Washington, 1983–1988.* Washington, D.C.: Metropolitan Washington Council of Governments, May.

———. 1989b. *Socio-Economic Implications of Growth Forecasts.* Washington, D.C.: Metropolitan Washington Council of Governments, February 8.

Miles, Jack. 1992. "Blacks Versus Browns." *Atlantic Monthly,* October, 41–68.

Mincer, Jacob. 1970. "The Distribution of Labor Incomes: A Survey with Special Reference to Human Capital Approach." *Journal of Economic Literature* 8:1–26.

Mines, Richard. 1984. "Network Migration and Mexican Rural Development: A Case Study." In *Patterns of Undocumented Migration:*

Mexico and the United States, ed. Richard Jones. Totowa, N.J.: Rowman & Allanheld.

Montes Mozo, Segundo, and Juan Jose Garcia Vasquez. 1988. *Salvadoran Migration to the United States: An Exploratory Study.* Washington, D.C.: Hemispheric Migration Project, Center for Immigration Policy and Refugee Assistance, Georgetown University.

Montgomery, Tommie Sue. 1982. *Revolution in El Salvador: Origins and Evolution.* Boulder, Colo.: Westview.

Morales, Rebecca. 1983. "Transitional Labor: Undocumented Workers in the Los Angeles Automobile Industry." *International Migration Review* 17, no.4:570–96.

Muller, Thomas, and Thomas Espenshade. 1985. *The Fourth Wave: California's Newest Immigrants.* Washington, D.C.: Urban Institute.

Nash, June. 1976. "A Critique of Social Sciences Roles in Latin America." In *Sex and Class in Latin America,* ed. June Nash and Helen Safa. New York: Praeger.

Nash, June, and Helen Safa, eds. 1976. *Sex and Class in Latin America.* New York: Praeger.

Nieves, Isabel. 1979. "Household Arrangements and Multiple Jobs in San Salvador." *Signs* 5, no.1:139.

Orlansky, Dora, and Silvia Dubrovsky. 1978. "The Effects of Rural-Urban Migration on Women's Roles and Status in Latin America." *Reports and Papers in the Social Sciences,* no. 41. New York: UNESCO.

Painter, James. 1987. *Guatemala: False Hope, False Freedom.* London: Catholic Institute for International Relations.

Papademetriou, Demetrios. 1990. "Contending Approaches to Reforming the U.S. Legal Immigration System." Paper prepared for the New York University/Rockefeller Foundation conference "Migration, Ethnicity, and the City," New York, November 2–4.

Pear, R. 1988. "Salvadoran Issues a Refugee Appeal." *New York Times,* September 11.

Pedraza, Silvia. 1992. "Cubans in Exile, 1959–1989: The State of Research." In *Cuban Studies Since the Revolution,* ed. Damian Fernandez. Gainesville: University Presses of Florida.

———. 1991. "Women and Migration: The Social Consequences of Gender." *Annual Review of Sociology* 17:303–25.

———. 1990. "Immigration Research: A Conceptual Map." *Social Science History* 14:43–68.

Pessar, Patricia. 1986. "The Role of Gender in Dominican Settlement in the United States." In *Women and Change in Latin America,* ed. June Nash and Helen Safa. South Hadley, Mass.: Bergin & Garvey.

———. 1984. "The Role of Households in International Migration and the Case of U.S.-Bound Migration from the Dominican Republic." *International Migration Review* 16:342–64.

Petuchowski, Silvia. 1988. *Psychological Adjustment Problems of War Refugees from El Salvador.* PhD. diss., University of Maryland.

Piore, Michael. 1979. *Birds of Passage: Migrant Labor and Industrial Societies.* New York: Cambridge University Press.

Poitras, Guy. 1980. *International Migration to the United States from Costa Rica and El Salvador.* San Antonio, Tex.: Border Research Institute.

Portes, Alejandro. 1983. "International Labor Migration and National Development." In *U.S. Immigration and Refugee Policy,* ed. Mary Kritz. Lexington, Mass.: D. C. Heath.

———. 1978a. "Migration and Underdevelopment." *Politics and Society* 8:1–48.

———. 1978b. "Toward a Structural Analysis of Illegal Immigration." *International Migration Review* 12:472.

Portes, Alejandro, and Robert Bach. 1985. *Latin Journey: Cuban and Mexican Immigrants in the United States.* Berkeley and Los Angeles: University of California Press.

———. 1980. "Immigrant Earnings: Cuban and Mexican Immigrants in the United States." *International Migration Review* 14:315–40.

Portes, Alejandro, and Ruben Rumbaut. 1990. *Immigrant America: A Portrait.* Berkeley and Los Angeles: University of California Press.

Power, Marilyn. 1990. "Occupational Mobility of Black and White Women Service Workers." Paper prepared for the Second Annual Women's Policy Research Conference, Institute for Women's Policy Research, Washington, D.C.

Pressley, Sue. 1987. "Area Melting Pot Getting Fuller." *Washington Post,* December 13.

Reimers, Cordelia. 1985. "A Comparative Analysis of the Wages of Hispanics, Blacks, and Non-Hispanic Whites." In *Hispanics in the U.S. Economy,* ed. George Borjas and Marta Tienda. New York: Academic Press.

Repak, Terry A. 1994a. "Labor Market Incorporation of Central American Immigrants in Washington, D.C." *Social Problems* 41:114–28.

———. 1994b. "Labor Recruitment and the Lure of the Capital: Central American Women in Washington, D.C." *Gender and Society* 8, no. 4:507–24.

———. 1990. "They Come on Behalf of Their Children: Central American Families in Washington, D.C." *Immigration Policy and Research Working Paper 3*. Washington, D.C.: U.S. Department of Labor, Bureau of International Labor Affairs.

Rich, Spencer. 1988. "Texas Cow County Is Nation's Richest." *Washington Post,* November 16.

Rodriguez, Nestor. 1987. "Undocumented Central Americans in Houston: Diverse Populations." *International Migration Review* 21:4–26.

Rollins, Judith. 1985. *Between Women: Domestics and Their Employers*. Philadelphia: Temple University Press.

Romero, Mary. 1992. *Maid in the U.S.A.* New York: Routledge.

———. 1988. "Day Work in the Suburbs: The Work Experience of Chicana Private Housekeepers." In *The Worth of Women's Work,* ed. Anne Statham et al. Albany: State University of New York Press.

Rubbo, Anna, and M. Taussig. 1978. "Up off Their Knees: Servanthood in Southwest Columbia." *Female Servants and Economic Development*. University of Michigan Occasional Papers in Women's Studies, no. 1. Ann Arbor: University of Michigan Press.

Ruggles, Patricia, and Michael Fix. 1985. "Impacts and Potential Impacts of Central American Migrants on HHS and Related Programs of Assistance." Final report prepared for the Office of the Assistant Secretary for Planning and Evaluation, U.S. Department of Health and Human Services, Washington, D.C.: Urban Institute.

Safa, Helen. 1979. "Multinationals and the Employment of Women in Developing Areas: The Case of the Caribbean." Graduate Department of Anthropology, Rutgers University. Mimeographed.

Salzinger, Leslie. 1991. "A Maid by Any Other Name: The Transformation of 'Dirty Work' by Central American Immigrants." In *Ethnography Unbound: Power and Resistance in the Modern Metropolis,* ed. Michael Buraway et al. Berkeley and Los Angeles: University of California Press.

Sassen-Koob, Saskia. 1986. "New York City: Economic Restructuring and Immigration." *Development and Change* 17:85–119.

————. 1984. "Notes on the Incorporation of Third World Women into Wage-Labor Through Immigration and Off-Shore Production." *International Migration Review* 18:1144–67.

Schulz, Thomas. 1989. *Statement from the U.S. General Accounting Office Before the U.S. Congressional Committee for the Study of International Migration and Cooperative Economic Development.* April 21.

Schultz, T. W. 1961. "Investment in Human Capital." *American Economic Review* 2:1–17.

Seager, Joni, and Ann Olson. 1986. *Women in the World: An International Atlas.* New York: Simon & Schuster.

Serafino, Nina. 1989. *Statement from the Congressional Research Service Before the U.S. Congressional Commission for the Study of International Migration and Cooperative Economic Development.* April 21.

Simon, Rita, and Margo DeLey. 1986. "Undocumented Mexican Women: Their Work and Personal Experiences." In *International Migration: The Female Experience,* ed. Rita Simon and Carolyn Brettell. Totowa, N.J.: Rowman & Allanheld.

————. 1984. "The Work Experience of Undocumented Mexican Women in Los Angeles." *International Migration Review* 18:1212–29.

Smith, Barbara. 1988. "Washington, D.C.: A Second Revolution." *Economist,* April 1.

Stanley, William. 1987. "Economic Migrants or Refugees from Violence? A Time-Series Analysis of Salvadoran Migration." *Latin American Research Review* 22:132–54.

Sullivan, Teresa. 1984. "The Occupational Prestige of Women Immigrants: A Comparison of Cubans and Mexicans." *International Migration Review* 18:1045–63.

Suro, R. 1989. "1986 Amnesty Law Is Seen As Failing to Slow Alien Tide." *New York Times,* June 18.

Theiler, P. 1985. "Double Standard." *Common Cause Magazine,* July.

Thomson, Marilyn. 1986. *Women of El Salvador: The Price of Freedom.* Philadelphia: Institute for the Study of Human Issues.

Tienda, Marta. 1983. "Socioeconomic and Labor Force Characteristics of U.S. Immigrants: Issues and Approaches." In *U.S. Immigration and Refugee Policy: Global and Domestic Issues,* ed. Mary Kritz. Lexington, Mass.: D. C. Heath.

Tienda, Marta, and Patricia Guhleman. 1985. "The Occupational Position of Employed Hispanic Women." In *Hispanics in the U.S. Economy,* ed. George Borjas and Marta Tienda. New York: Academic Press.

Tienda, Marta, et al. 1984. "Immigration, Gender, and the Process of Occupational Change in the United States, 1970–80." *International Migration Review* 18:1021.

Tilly, Charles. 1978. "Migration in Modern European History." In *Human Migration: Patterns and Policies,* ed. William H. McNeill and Ruth S. Adams. Bloomington: Indiana University Press.

Todaro, Michael. 1977. *Economic Development in the Third World.* New York: Longman.

Torres-Rivas, Edelberto. 1984. "Problems of Democracy and Counterrevolution in Guatemala." In *Political Change in Central America,* ed. Wolf Grabendorff and Heinrich Krumwiede. Boulder, Colo.: Westview.

United Nations. 1979. *Trends and Characteristics of International Migration Since 1950.* New York: United Nations.

UNICEF. 1982. *Dimensions of Poverty in Latin America and the Caribbean.* Washington, D.C.: United Nations.

U.S. Committee for Refugees. 1984. *Aiding the Desplazados of El Salvador: The Complexity of Humanitarian Assistance.* Washington, D.C.: U.S. Committee for Refugees.

U.S. Congress. 1992. *Immigration and Nationality Act.*

U.S. Congress, Arms Control and Foreign Policy Caucus. 1985. *U.S. Aid to El Salvador: An Evaluation of the Past, A Proposal for the Future.* Washington, D.C.: GPO.

U.S. Department of Labor. 1991. *Employer Sanctions and U.S. Labor Markets: Final Report.* Washington, D.C.: Division of Immigration Policy and Research, U.S. Department of Labor.

U.S. General Accounting Office (GAO). 1989. *Central America: Conditions of Refugees and Displaced Persons.* Washington, D.C.: GPO.

———. 1988. *Illegal Aliens: Influence of Illegal Workers on Wages and Working Conditions of Legal Workers.* Report to U.S. Congress.

U.S. Immigration and Naturalization Service. 1986. *Handbook for Employers: Instructions for Completing Form I-9.* Washington, D.C.: U.S. Department of Justice.

Van Dyne, Larry. 1984. "Halfway to Heaven." *Washingtonian,* May.

Verdugo, Naomi. 1982. *The Effects of Discrimination on the Earnings of Hispanic Workers: Findings and Policy Implications*. Washington, D.C.: National Council of La Raza.

Wachtel, H. M. 1972. "Capitalism and Poverty in America: Paradox or Contradiction?" *American Economic Review* 62:187–94.

Wallace, Steven P. 1986. "Central American and Mexican Immigrant Characteristics and Economic Incorporation in California." *International Migration Review* 20:657–71.

Washington-Baltimore Regional Association. 1989. *The Baltimore-Washington Common Market: Economic Profile*. Washington, D.C.: Washington-Baltimore Regional Association.

————. 1987. "Washington Area Is Leading the Nation in Income and Education." *Washington Post,* July 26.

Webre, Stephen. 1986. "The Ideology of Salvadoran Christian Democracy." In *El Salvador: Central America in the New Cold War,* ed. Marvin Gettleman et al. New York: Grove Press.

Wilkinson, Tracy. 1993. "Officials, Death Squads Get Most Salvadoran Blame." *New York Times,* March 16.

Williams, Brett. 1988. *Upscaling Downtown: Stalled Gentrification in Washington, D.C.* Ithaca, N.Y.: Cornell University Press.

Williams, Robert. 1986. *Export Agriculture and the Crisis in Central America*. Chapel Hill: University of North Carolina Press.

Wood, Charles. 1982. "Equilibrium and Historical-Structural Perspectives in Migration." *International Migration Review* 16:298–319.

Woodward, Ralph. 1985. *Central America: A Nation Divided*. 2d ed. New York: Oxford University Press.

Zhou, Min, and John Logan. 1989. "Returns on Human Capital in Ethnic Enclaves: New York City's Chinatown." *American Sociological Review* 54:809–20.

Zolberg, Aristide, Astri Surke, and Sergio Aguayo. 1986. "International Factors in the Formation of Refugee Movements." *International Migration Review* 20:151–69.

Index